D1037394

ING
FO-C-IEC.
1496009

Teaching
Students
With
Learning Disabilities

This book is dedicated to my wife, Jackie, and my two children, Jacqueline and Scott, who provide me with the love and purpose for undertaking projects that I hope will enhance the lives of others. My life has been blessed by their loving presence.
I also dedicate this book to my parents, who provided me with the secure and loving foundation from which to grow; my sister, Carol, who makes me smile and laugh; and my brother-in-law, George, who has always been a positive guiding light in my professional journey.

—R. P.

This book is dedicated to my wife, Anita, and two children, Collin and Brittany, who give me the greatest life imaginable. The long hours and many years it took to finish this book would never have been possible without the support of my loving wife. Her constant encouragement, understanding, and love provide me with the strength I need to accomplish my goals. I thank her with all my heart. I also dedicate this book to my parents, who have given me support and guidance throughout my life. Their words of encouragement and guidance have made my professional journey a rewarding and successful experience.

—G. G.

A STEP-BY-STEP GUIDE FOR EDUCATORS

Teaching Students With Learning Disabilities

ROGER PIERANGELO ~ GEORGE GIULIANI

CORWIN PRESS
A SAGE Company
Thousand Oaks, CA 91320

Copyright © 2008 by Corwin Press

All rights reserved. When forms and sample documents are included, their use is authorized only by educators, local school sites, and/or noncommercial or nonprofit entities that have purchased the book. Except for that usage, no part of this book may be reproduced or utilized in any form or by any means, electronic or mechanical, including photocopying, recording, or by any information storage and retrieval system, without permission in writing from the publisher.

For information:

Corwin Press
A SAGE Company
2455 Teller Road
Thousand Oaks, California 91320
www.corwinpress.com

SAGE Ltd.
1 Oliver's Yard
55 City Road
London EC1Y 1SP
United Kingdom

SAGE India Pvt. Ltd.
B 1/I 1 Mohan Cooperative
   Industrial Area
Mathura Road, New Delhi 110 044
India

SAGE Asia-Pacific Pte. Ltd.
33 Pekin Street #02-01
Far East Square
Singapore 048763

Printed in the United States of America.

Library of Congress Cataloging-in-Publication Data

Pierangelo, Roger.
Teaching students with learning disabilities: a step-by-step guide for educators / Roger Pierangelo and George Giuliani.
        p. cm.
Includes bibliographical references and index.
ISBN 978-1-4129-1600-4 (cloth)
ISBN 978-1-4129-1601-1 (pbk.)
    1. Learning disabled children—Education—United States. 2. Special education—United States. I. Giuliani, George A., 1938- II. Title.

LC4705.P497 2008
371.9—dc22   2008001268

This book is printed on acid-free paper.

08   09   10   11   12   10 9 8 7 6 5 4 3 2 1

Acquisitions Editor:	David Chao
Editorial Assistant:	Mary Dang
Production Editor:	Libby Larson
Copy Editor:	Paula L. Fleming
Typesetter:	C&M Digitals (P) Ltd.
Proofreader:	Theresa Kay
Cover Designer:	Michael Dubowe
Graphic Designer:	Lisa Riley

Contents

Preface   x

Acknowledgments   xiii

About the Authors   xv

1. Overview of Learning Disabilities   1
  IDEA Definition of a Specific Learning Disability   1
  Overview of Specific Learning Disabilities   2
  Key Facts About Learning Disabilities   3
  Causes of a Specific Learning Disability   4
    Genetics   4
    Tobacco, Alcohol, and Other Drug
      Use During Pregnancy   5
    Complications During Pregnancy   6
    Environmental Toxins   6
    Mercury Poisoning   6
    Lead Poisoning   6
    Poor Nutrition   7
    Maturational Delay   7
  Prevalence of Specific Learning Disabilities   7
  Age of Onset for Specific Learning Disabilities   8
  Gender Features for Specific Learning Disabilities   8
  Cultural Features for Specific Learning Disabilities   8
  Familial Patterns for Specific Learning Disabilities   8
  Comorbidity for Specific Learning Disabilities   9
  "Discrepancy" in Diagnosing a Learning Disability   9
  The Exclusionary Clause   10
  Characteristics of Specific Learning Disabilities   11
  Educational Implications of Specific Learning Disabilities   12

2. Characteristics of Children With Learning Disabilities   **14**

Academic Achievement Deficits   16
Reading   16
     Oral Reading   17
     Reading Comprehension   20
     Word Recognition Skills   21
     Reading Habits   22
Math   22
     Analysis and Interpretation of Math Skills   23
Written Expression   25
     Handwriting   26
     Spelling   26
Language Deficits   29
     Oral Language Problems   29
     Listening Comprehension Problems   30
     Problems With Pragmatics   30
Disorders of Attention   31
Achievement Discrepancy   31
Memory Deficits   32
Cognitive Deficits   34
Metacognition Deficits   34
Social-Emotional Problems   35
Nonverbal Learning Disorders (NLD)   38
Motivational and Attribution Problems   39
Perceptual Deficits   40

3. Types of Learning Disabilities   **41**

Auditory Processing Disorders   41
Dyscalculia (Arithmetic Disorders)   42
Dysgraphia (Writing Disorders)   44
Dyslexia (Reading Disorders)   45
Dysorthographia (Spelling Disorders)   46
Nonverbal Learning Disabilities (NLD)   47
Organizational Learning Disorders   48
Social Cue Disorder   49
Visual Processing Disorders   50

4. Eligibility Criteria for Learning Disabilities   **52**

Step I: Becoming Familiar With the Characteristics
     of Students With Specific Learning Disabilities   52
Step II: Determining the Procedures and
     Assessment Measures to Be Used   53
Step III: Determination of Eligibility for a
     Diagnosis of a Specific Learning Disability   55

Option 1   55
Option 2   56
Key Points to Remember When Determining
    Eligibility for LD   58

5. Response to Intervention (RTI)   **59**
Purpose of RTI   60
Importance of RTI   61
Is RTI a "New Approach"?   62
Core Principles of RTI   62
Events That Led to Changes in LD
    Identification in IDEA 2004   65
Rationale for Replacing the Discrepancy Model With RTI   66
Major Issues Related to the Use of the Concept
    of Achievement-Ability Discrepancy   66
Why RTI Was Considered in the Process
    of LD Determination   67
The Role RTI Should Play in the Identification
    of Children With Specific Learning Disabilities   68
Can RTI Be Used as the Sole Determinant
    for LD Classification?   69
In the Big Picture, How Does RTI Fit Into the
    Process of Determining LD?   70
Multitiered Service Delivery Model   72
    Focus of Tier I   75
    Focus of Tier II   75
    Focus of Tier III   75
Parent Involvement: An Important Component
    of Successful RTI Programs   76
Fidelity   77
The RTI Process for Teachers   77
What Teachers Need in Terms of Professional
    Development and RTI   78

6. Effective Teaching Strategies for Students With LD   **80**
Academic Instruction   80
    Prepare Students for Upcoming Lessons   80
    Conducting Effective Lessons   81
    Concluding Lessons   84
    Individualizing Instructional Practices   84
    Organizational and Study Skills Useful for
        Academic Instruction of Students With LD   89
    Assisting Students With LD With Time Management   90
    Helpful Study Skills for Students With LD   90

Behavioral Interventions 91
    Effective Behavioral Intervention Techniques 92
Classroom Accommodations 96
    Special Classroom Seating Arrangements
       for LD Students 97
    Instructional Tools and the Physical
       Learning Environment 97

**7. Promoting Positive Social Interactions in
an Inclusion Setting 99**
Review of Inclusion 100
Principles of Effective Inclusion 100
Why Are Social Skills Important? 101
Social-Cognitive Skill Development 102
The Role of Social Skills at School 102
Strategies to Foster a Sense of Belonging in the
    Inclusion Classroom 103
Creating a Positive Inclusion Classroom Climate 104
Teaching Social Skills Through Role-Playing
    and Observation 105
The Inclusion Classroom Teacher's Power
    to Model Acceptance 106
Promoting Positive Interactions 106
    Conduct Class Meetings 107
    Use Values Clarification 107
    Project a Feeling, Caring Persona 107
    Use Reprimands Judiciously 108
    Validate Student Feelings 108
    Post Positive Behavior 109
    Promote Self-Monitoring 109
    Train for Generalization 109
    Deal Appropriately With Name-Calling and Teasing 109
    Offer Choices and Solicit Preferences 110
    Promote Self-Esteem 110
    Provide Attribution Training 110
    Demonstrate or Model Rules and Procedures;
       Then Allow Students to Rehearse Them 111
    With Older Students, Use Contingency Contracts 111

**8. IEP Development and Educational Placement
Options for Students With Learning Disabilities 112**
Members of the IEP Committee 112
Responsibilities of the IEP Committee 113
IDEA 2004 and IEP Committee Meetings: What to Know 115
Development of the Information Packet for
    Presentation to the IEP Committee 115

Required Forms	116
Evaluations (Initial Referral)	117
Guidance and School Materials (Initial Referral)	117
Other Materials	118
How Recommendations for Classification Are Made by the IEP Committee	121
Specific Educational Placement (LRE) Considerations According to IDEA 2004	121
Appealing the Decision of the IEP Committee	126
Other Roles of the IEP Committee	127
Special Meetings	127
Annual Review	127
Triennial Review	129
Declassification Procedures of a Child in Special Education	129
IEP Development	130
Components to Be Included in the IEP	131
Questions and Answers About the IEP Under IDEA 2004	131
Conclusion	136
9. Transition Services for Students With Learning Disabilities	**138**
The Transitional Process	138
The Intent of Transition Services	140
The Importance of Transition Services for Individuals With Learning Disabilities	140
The Introduction of Transition Services	140
The Individualized Transition Plan (ITP)	141
Transition Services	142
Special Considerations for Students With Learning Disabilities	143
Employment Services	144
Leisure/Recreational Experiences	147
Postsecondary Education Options	148
When to Begin College Planning	150
Understanding Legal Rights Pertaining to Postsecondary Education	151
Identifying the Desirable Characteristics of a College	151
Disability-Related Support Services	154
Assistive Technology	154
Glossary	**159**
References	**162**
Index	**172**

Preface

Learning disability is a general term that describes specific kinds of learning problems. A learning disability can cause a person to have trouble learning and using certain skills. The skills most often affected are reading, writing, listening, speaking, reasoning, and doing math.

Learning disabilities (LD) vary from person to person. One person with LD may not have the same kind of learning problems as another person with LD.

Researchers think that learning disabilities are caused by differences in how a person's brain works and how it processes information. Children with learning disabilities are not "dumb" or "lazy." In fact, they usually have average or above-average intelligence. Their brains just process information differently.

There is no "cure" for learning disabilities. They are life long. However, children with LD can be high achievers and can be taught ways to get around the learning disability. With the right help, children with LD can and do learn successfully.

There is no *one* sign that shows a person has a learning disability. Experts look for a noticeable difference between how well a child does in school and how well the child *could* do, given his or her intelligence or ability. Also, certain clues may indicate that a child has a learning disability. We've listed a few below. Most relate to elementary school tasks, because learning disabilities tend to be identified in elementary school. A child probably won't show all of these signs or even most of them. However, if a child shows a number of these problems, then parents and the teacher should consider the possibility that the child has a learning disability.

A child with a learning disability may have challenges with the following tasks:

- Learning the alphabet, rhyming words, or connecting letters to their sounds
- Reading aloud, making many mistakes and repeating and pausing often

- Understanding what is read
- Spelling
- Writing neatly, possibly holding a pencil awkwardly
- Expressing ideas in writing
- Learning language, picking it up late and having a limited vocabulary
- Remembering the sounds that letters make or hearing slight differences between words
- Understanding jokes, comic strips, and sarcasm
- Following directions
- Pronouncing words correctly or using the correct word when another sounds similar
- Organizing what he or she wants to say or thinking of the word needed for writing or conversation
- Following the social rules of conversation, such as taking turns or not standing too close to the listener
- Confusing math symbols and misreading numbers
- Retelling a story in order (what happened first, second, third)
- Knowing where to begin a task or how to go on from there

If a child has unexpected problems learning to read, write, listen, speak, or do math, then teachers and parents may want to investigate more. The same is true if the child is struggling to do any one of these skills. The child may need to be evaluated to see if there is a learning disability.

Learning disabilities tend to be diagnosed when children reach school age. This is because school focuses on the very things that may be difficult for the child—reading, writing, math, listening, speaking, and reasoning. Teachers and parents notice that the child is not learning as expected. The school may ask to evaluate the child to see what is causing the problem. Parents can also ask for their child to be evaluated.

With hard work and the proper help, children with LD can learn more easily and successfully. For school-aged children (including preschoolers), special education and related services are important sources of help. School staff members work with the child's parents to develop an individualized education program, or IEP. This document describes the child's unique needs. It also describes the special education services that will be provided to meet those needs. These services are provided at no cost to the child or family.

Teaching Students With Learning Disabilities: A Step-by-Step Guide for Educators is intended to provide educators with a step-by-step approach to the most effective methods of teaching students with learning disabilities.

Teaching Students With Learning Disabilities: A Step-by-Step Guide for Educators was written to explain learning disabilities through the eyes of the teacher, so that if a student in your class or school is diagnosed with learning disabilities, you can work effectively with administrators, parents, other professionals, and the outside community to provide that child with the best education possible.

We hope that *Teaching Students With Learning Disabilities: A Step-by-Step Guide for Educators* will be helpful to you in understanding the key concepts of this exceptionality and how to be an effective educator when working with students diagnosed with learning disabilities.

Acknowledgments

In the course of writing this book, we have encountered many professional and outstanding sites. Those resources have contributed and continue to contribute enormous information, support, guidance, and education to parents, students, and professionals in the area of special education. Although we have accessed many worthwhile sites, we especially thank and acknowledge the National Dissemination Center for Children with Disabilities, the U.S. Department of Education, and the National Institutes of Health.

Both Dr. Pierangelo and Dr. Giuliani extend sincere thanks to Allyson Sharpe, Paula Fleming, Mary Dang, Libby Larson, and Laureen Shea for all of their hard work and dedication toward making this book a reality. We could not have completed it without your constant support and encouragement. They would also like to thank the following for their professional contributions to the book:

Janette Bowen
Teacher (6th Grade CWC/SPED)
Junction City Middle School
Junction City, KS

Esther Eacho
Special Education Teacher
Fairfax County Public Schools
Falls Church, VA

Alyssa Carter
Administrator of Federal
    Programs
Kuna Jt. School District No. 3
Kuna, ID

Carolyn Guess
Assistant Superintendent
    for SPED
Houston Independent School
    District
Houston, TX

Roger Pierangelo: I extend thanks to the following: the faculty, administration, and staff of the Department of Graduate Special Education and Literacy at Long Island University; Ollie Simmons, for her friendship, loyalty, and great personality; the students and parents of the Herricks Public Schools whom I have worked with and known over the past 35 years; the late Bill Smyth, a truly gifted and "extraordinary ordinary" man; and Helen Firestone, for her influence on my career and her tireless support.

George Giuliani: I extend sincere thanks to all of my colleagues at Hofstra University in the School of Education and Allied Human Services. I am especially grateful to those who have made my transition to Hofstra University such a smooth one, including Maureen Murphy (dean), Darra Pace (chairperson), Frank Bowe, Diane Schwartz (graduate program director of early childhood special education), Daniel Sciarra, Gloria Wilson, Laurie Johnson, Joan Bloomgarden, Jamie Mitus, Estelle Gellman, Joseph Lechowicz, Holly Seirup, Adele Piombino, Marjorie Butler, and Eve Byrne. I also thank my brother and sister, Roger and Claudia; my mother-in-law, Ursula Jenkeleit; my sisters-in-law, Karen and Cindy; and my brothers-in-law, Robert and Bob. They have provided me with encouragement and reinforcement in all of my personal and professional endeavors.

About the Authors

Dr. Roger Pierangelo, PhD, is an associate professor in the Department of Special Education and Literacy at Long Island University. He has been an administrator of special education programs; served for 18 years as a permanent member of Committees on Special Education; has over 30 years of experience in the public school system as a general education classroom teacher and school psychologist; and serves as a consultant to numerous private and public schools, PTA, and SEPTA groups. Dr. Pierangelo has also been an evaluator for the New York State Office of Vocational and Rehabilitative Services and a director of a private clinic. He is a New York State–licensed clinical psychologist, a certified school psychologist, and a Board Certified Diplomate Fellow in Student and Adolescent Psychology and Forensic Psychology. Dr. Pierangelo is the executive director of the National Association of Special Education Teachers (NASET) and an executive director of the American Academy of Special Education Professionals (AASEP). He also holds the office of vice president of the National Association of Parents with Children in Special Education (NAPCSE).

Dr. Pierangelo earned his BS from St. John's University, MS from Queens College, Professional Diploma from Queens College, PhD from Yeshiva University, and Diplomate Fellow in Student and Adolescent Psychology and Forensic Psychology from the International College of Professional Psychology. Dr. Pierangelo is a member of the American Psychological Association, New York State Psychological Association, Nassau County Psychological Association, New York State Union of Teachers, and Phi Delta Kappa.

Dr. Pierangelo is the coauthor of multiple books by Corwin Press, including *The Big Book of Special Education Resources* and the *Step-by-Step Guide for Educators* series.

Dr. George Giuliani, JD, PsyD, is a full-time tenured associate professor and the director of Special Education at Hofstra University's School of Education and Allied Human Services in the Department of Counseling, Research, Special Education, and Rehabilitation. Dr. Giuliani earned his BA from the College of the Holy Cross, MS from St. John's University, JD from City University Law School, and PsyD from Rutgers University, the Graduate School of Applied and Professional Psychology. He earned Board Certification as a Diplomate Fellow in Student and Adolescent Psychology and Forensic Psychology from the International College of Professional Psychology. Dr. Giuliani is also a New York State–licensed psychologist and certified school psychologist and has an extensive private practice focusing on students with special needs. He is a member of the American Psychological Association, New York State Psychological Association, National Association of School Psychologists, Suffolk County Psychological Association, Psi Chi, American Association of University Professors, and the Council for Exceptional Students.

Dr. Giuliani is the president of the National Association of Parents with Children in Special Education (NAPCSE), executive director of the National Association of Special Education Teachers (NASET), and executive director of the American Academy of Special Education Professionals (AASEP). He is a consultant for school districts and early childhood agencies and has provided numerous workshops for parents and guardians and teachers on a variety of special education and psychological topics. Dr. Giuliani is the coauthor of numerous books by Corwin Press, including *The Big Book of Special Education Resources* and the *Step-by-Step Guide for Educators* series.

1

Overview of Learning Disabilities

IDEA Definition of a Specific Learning Disability

Under the Individuals with Disabilities Education Act of 2004 (IDEA), the federal law that protects students with disabilities, a *specific learning disability* is defined as

> (i) General. The term means a disorder in one or more of the basic psychological processes involved in understanding or in using language, spoken or written, that may manifest itself in an imperfect ability to listen, think, speak, read, write, spell, or to do mathematical calculations, including conditions such as perceptual disabilities, brain injury, minimal brain dysfunction, dyslexia, and developmental aphasia.
>
> (ii) Disorders not included. The term does not include learning problems that are primarily the result of visual, hearing, or motor disabilities, of mental retardation, of emotional disturbance, or of environmental, cultural, or economic disadvantage. (34 C.F.R. 300.7[c][10])

Note that the definition of "a specific learning disability" under IDEA 2004 remains unchanged from that in IDEA of 1997. However, under the new provisions in IDEA 2004, a local educational agency is not required to take into consideration whether a child has a severe discrepancy between achievement and intellectual ability in oral expression, listening comprehension, written expression, basic reading skill, reading comprehension, mathematical calculation or mathematical reasoning. In determining whether a child has a specific learning disability, a local educational agency may use a process that determines if a child responds to scientific, research-based intervention as a part of the evaluation procedures. (34 C.F.R. § 300.541)

Overview of Specific Learning Disabilities

On April 6, 1963, the term *learning disabilities* was coined by Professor Sam Kirk and others at a meeting of parents and professionals in Chicago (Pierangelo & Giuliani, 2006). In 1975, the disability category "Specific Learning Disability" was first included in the federal law, P.L. 94–142, the Education for All Handicapped Children Act (Hunt & Marshall, 2005).

In general, *learning disabilities* refers to a neurobiological disorder related to differences in how one's brain works and is structured. Further, learning disability is a general term that describes specific kinds of learning problems. A learning disability can cause a person to have trouble learning and using certain skills (Lerner, 2002). The skills most often affected are reading, writing, listening, speaking, reasoning, and doing math (Heward, 2005; National Dissemination Center for Children with Disabilities, 2004; Pierangelo & Giuliani, 2006).

Learning disabilities (LD) vary from person to person and encompass a heterogeneous group of disorders. One person with LD may not have the same kind of learning problems as another person with LD. Someone with LD may have problems with understanding math. Another person may have trouble understanding what people are saying. Therefore, no single profile of an individual with LD can be accurate because of the inter-individual differences in the disorder (Friend, 2005).

Children with learning disabilities are not "dumb" or "lazy." In fact, they usually have average or above-average intelligence. Their brains just process information differently (Gargiulo, 2004). The general belief among researchers is that learning disabilities exist because of some type of dysfunction in the brain, not because of external factors such as limited experience or poor teaching (Friend, 2005; Hallahan & Kauffman, 2006).

Key Facts About Learning Disabilities

To understand the impact learning disabilities have on children and young adults in the United States, it's helpful to look at some key statistics:

- Nearly 2.9 million students are currently receiving special education services for learning disabilities in the United States (U.S. Department of Education, 2002).
- Approximately 50 percent of students receiving special education services through the public schools are identified as having learning disabilities (U.S. Department of Education, 2004).
- The majority (around 85 percent) of all individuals with learning disabilities have difficulties in the area of reading (President's Commission on Excellence in Special Education, 2002).
- Two-thirds of secondary students with learning disabilities are reading three or more grade levels behind. Twenty percent are reading five or more grade levels behind (The Achievements of Youth with Disabilities During Secondary School, National Longitudinal Transition Study-2, 2003, cited in National Center for Learning Disabilities, 2004).
- Of parents who noticed their child exhibiting signs of difficulty with learning, 44 percent waited a year or more before acknowledging their child might have a serious problem (Roper Starch Poll: Measuring Progress in Public and Parental Understanding of Learning Disabilities, 2000, cited in National Center for Learning Disabilities, 2004).
- More than 27 percent of children with learning disabilities drop out of high school, compared to 11 percent of the general student population (U.S. Department of Education, 2002).
- Two-thirds of high school graduates with learning disabilities were rated "not qualified" to enter a four-year college, compared to 37 percent of nondisabled graduates (Students with Disabilities in Postsecondary Education: A Profile of Preparation, Participation, and Outcomes, NCES, 1999, cited in National Center for Learning Disabilities, 2004).
- Only 13 percent of students with learning disabilities (compared to 53 percent of students in general population) have attended a four-year postsecondary school program within two years of leaving high school (National Longitudinal Transition Study, 1994, cited in National Center for Learning Disabilities, 2004).

- There is no causal link between learning disabilities and substance abuse. However, the risk factors for adolescent substance abuse are very similar to the behavioral effects of LD, such as reduced self-esteem and academic difficulty (National Center for Addiction and Substance Abuse, 1999, cited in National Center for Learning Disabilities, 2004).
- Of all students with disabilities enrolled at postsecondary education institutions, 46 percent reported having LD. In public two-year institutions, 38 percent of all students with disabilities have LD. At public four-year institutions, 51 percent of students with disabilities have LD (National Center for Education Statistics, 1999, cited in National Center for Learning Disabilities, 2004).
- Since 1992, the percentage of students with learning disabilities who spend more than 80 percent of their instructional time in general education has more than doubled, from 21 percent to 45 percent (U.S. Department of Education, 2002).
- Learning disabilities are not the same as mental retardation, autism, hearing or visual impairment, physical disabilities, emotional disorders, or the normal process of learning a second language.
- Learning disabilities aren't caused by a lack of educational opportunities, such as frequent changes of schools, poor school attendance, or lack of instruction in basic skills.

Causes of a Specific Learning Disability

Despite intense research activity over the years, pinpointing the precise cause or causes of learning disabilities has remained an elusive goal (Deutsch-Smith, 2004; Turnbull, Turnbull, Shank, & Smith, 2004).

Once, scientists thought that all learning disabilities were due to the effects of a single neurological problem (Hallahan & Kauffman, 2006). Today, research indicates that the causes are more diverse and complex (Pierangelo & Giuliani, 2006). New evidence seems to show that most learning disabilities do not stem from a single, specific area of the brain but from difficulties in bringing together information from various brain regions (Lerner, 2002; University of Maryland Medical Center, 2004).

Research has suggested various possible causes for specific learning disabilities.

Genetics

Over the years, evidence has accumulated that learning disabilities can be inherited (Hallahan & Kauffman, 2006). The fact that learning disabilities tend to run in families indicates a possible genetic link (Winkler, 2006). Researchers have found that about 35 to 45 percent of first-degree relatives—that is, the immediate birth family (parents and siblings)—of persons with reading disabilities have reading disabilities. Twin studies have shown that if one twin has a reading disability, the probability of the other twin's also having a reading disability is 68 percent for identical twins (monozygotic) and 40 percent for fraternal twins (dizygotic). The research evidence generally supports the hypothesis that certain types of learning problems, including reading disabilities, are more common among identical twins than fraternal twins. Some experts are beginning to suggest that an interactive relationship among several genes establishes the risk factors for reading disabilities (Wood & Grigorenko, 2001). Similar findings are also observed in twins with speech and language disorders (Wood & Grigorenko).

Tobacco, Alcohol, and Other Drug Use During Pregnancy

Research shows that a mother's use of cigarettes, alcohol, or other drugs during pregnancy may have damaging effects on the unborn child (Centers for Disease Control and Prevention, 2001; Roy, 1994; Wakschlag, Lahey, & Loeber, 1997).

Scientists have found that mothers who smoke during pregnancy may be more likely to bear smaller babies. This is a concern because small newborns, usually those weighing less than five pounds, tend to be at risk for a variety of problems, including learning disorders (Centers for Disease Control and Prevention, 2001; Roy, 1994; Wakschlag et al., 1997).

Alcohol also may be dangerous to the fetus' developing brain (Coles et al., 1991; Dumas, 1994; Gusella & Fried, 1984; Hanson, 1992; Kennedy & Mukerji, 1986; Lucchi & Covelli, 1984; Mattson et al., 1994; Mayo Clinic Staff, 2007b; Rawat, 1977; Shaywitz & Cohen 1980; Streissguth, Barr, & Sampson, 1986; Sulik, Johnston, & Webb, 1981). It appears that alcohol may distort the developing neurons. Any alcohol use during pregnancy may influence the child's development and lead to problems with learning, attention, memory, or problem solving.

The extensive use of drugs like marijuana and cocaine has been associated with increases in symptoms associated with learning disabilities (Abel, 1985; Fried & Smith, 2001; Fried & Watkinson, 1992). Because children with certain learning disabilities have difficulty understanding speech sounds or letters, some researchers believe that learning disabilities, as well as ADHD, may be related to faulty receptors. Current research points to drug abuse as a possible cause of receptor damage.

Complications During Pregnancy

Other possible causes of learning disabilities involve complications during pregnancy (University of Maryland Medical Center, 2004). In some cases, the mother's immune system reacts to the fetus and attacks it as if it were an infection. This type of disruption seems to cause newly formed brain cells to settle in the wrong part of the brain. Or during delivery, the umbilical cord may become twisted and temporarily cut off oxygen to the fetus. This, too, can impair brain functions and lead to LD.

Low-birth-weight babies are at risk for learning disabilities. According to some studies, children whose birth weight was less than two lbs. (800 grams) lagged behind their peers academically and displayed other subtle behavioral characteristics that undermined their efforts at school. Poor motor skills and neurological immaturity were found in many of these preschool-age children (Learning Disabilities Association of British Columbia, 1997/1998).

Environmental Toxins

New brain cells and neural networks continue to be produced for a year or so after the child is born. Like fetal cells, these cells are also vulnerable to certain disruptions. Researchers are looking into environmental toxins that may lead to learning disabilities, possibly by disrupting childhood brain development or brain processes (Neuwirth, 1999).

Mercury Poisoning

Mercury, all-prevalent in the environment, is becoming a leading focus of neurological research (Echeverria, Heyer, Martin, & Naleway, 1995; Emory, Patillo, Archibold, Bayorh, & Sung, 1999; Leong, Syed, & Lorscheider, 2001). Mercury, like lead, is particularly harmful to children. Mercury exposure can result in lowered intelligence, learning problems, birth defects, and brain damage.

Lead Poisoning

Approximately 434,000 U.S. children aged one to five years have blood lead levels greater than the Centers for Disease Control and Prevention's (2004) recommended level of 10 micrograms of lead per deciliter of blood. Lead was once common in paint and gasoline and is still present in some water pipes. Children under the age of six are especially vulnerable to lead's harmful health effects, because their brains and central nervous systems are still being formed. For them, even very low levels of exposure can result in reduced IQ, learning disabilities, attention deficit disorders, behavioral problems, stunted growth, impaired hearing, and kidney damage (National Safety Council, 2004).

Poor Nutrition

There seems to be a link between nutritional deprivation and poor biochemical functioning in the brain. A poor diet and severe malnutrition can reduce the child's ability to learn by damaging intersensory abilities and delaying development. Studies over the past ten years and clinical trials (conducted at Purdue University in the United States and Surrey and Oxford in the United Kingdom) indicate that some learning disabilities may have a nutritional basis. Other studies indicate that some learning disabilities might be caused by allergies to certain foods, food additives, and dyes or environmental allergies (Pierangelo & Giuliani, 2006).

Maturational Delay

Another theory to explain learning disabilities suggests that they occur because of maturational delay—rather than permanent dysfunction—within the neurological system.

Prevalence of Specific Learning Disabilities

According to the *26th Annual Report to Congress on the Implementation of Individuals with Disabilities Education Act* (U.S. Department of Education, 2004), 2,816,361 students between the ages of 6 to 21 were identified as having specific learning disabilities. This represents approximately 47 percent of all students having a classification in special education, or about 5 percent of all school-age students.

There are many conflicting reports on the actual number of individuals with specific learning disabilities. Since 1976–1977, when the federal government first started keeping prevalence figures, the size of the specific learning disability category has more than doubled (Hallahan & Kauffman, 2006), while the number of students identified as having a specific learning disability has grown by over 250 percent, from approximately 800,000 students to almost three million (U.S. Department of Education, 2004).

Learning disabilities has also been the fastest growing category of special education since the federal law was passed in 1975. Furthermore, the number of students with learning disabilities has increased almost 30 percent in the past nine years, a rate of growth much greater than the overall rate of growth for the number of students in school (Friend, 2005).

Age of Onset for Specific Learning Disabilities

Some forms of learning disabilities become apparent in preschool, while others might not be apparent until later in elementary school or even middle school. The number of students increases steadily between the ages of six and nine, which is not surprising considering the increasing academic demands of the elementary school curriculum. The bulk of students served (42 percent), however, are between the ages of 10 and 13, with a sharp decrease observed for individuals between 16 and 21 (U.S. Department of Education, 2000, cited in Gargiulo, 2004, p. 211).

Gender Features for Specific Learning Disabilities

The matter of gender and LD is one of controversy among researchers in the field. Although some studies have indicated that the prevalence of learning disabilities is equally distributed between males and females (Alexander, Gray, & Lyon, 1993), a number of researchers have found that the ratio of boys to girls identified as having learning disabilities is 3:1 (Hallahan & Kauffman, 2006), 4:1 (Gargiulo, 2004; Lerner, 2002), or even higher (Lyon, 1997; McLeskey, 1992).

Cultural Features for Specific Learning Disabilities

The 1997 IDEA amendments mandated that states collect special education "child count" data by race/ethnicity, beginning with the 1998–1999 school year. The U.S. Department of Education (2000) reported special education identification rates by race/ethnicity and disability for children ages 6 through 21. According to this report, 4.27 percent of White children were identified as having LD; corresponding figures for other race/ethnicity groups were as follows: American Indian/Alaska native, 6.29 percent; Black, 5.67 percent; Hispanic, 4.97 percent; and Asian/Pacific Islander, 1.7 percent.

Familial Patterns for Specific Learning Disabilities

The fact that learning disabilities tend to run in families indicates that there may be a genetic link (Bishop et al., 2003; Davis, Knopik, Olson,

Wadsworth, & DeFries, 2001; Kaplan et al., 2002; Knopik et al., 2002; Wadsworth, Corley, Hewitt, Plomin, & DeFries, 2002). For example, children who lack some of the skills needed for reading, such as hearing the separate sounds of words, are likely to have a parent with a related problem. However, a parent's learning disability may take a slightly different form in the child. A parent who has a writing disorder may have a child with an expressive language disorder. For this reason, it seems unlikely that specific learning disorders are inherited directly. Possibly what is inherited is a subtle brain dysfunction that can, in turn, lead to a learning disability.

Comorbidity for Specific Learning Disabilities

According to Chandler (2004), *comorbidity* means that certain diseases and disorders tend to occur together. For example, heart disease and stroke often occur in the same person. Many neuropsychiatric disorders tend to occur together. About 50 percent of children with learning disabilities have another neuropsychiatric disorder (Jongmans, Smits-Engelsman, & Schoemaker, 2003). Assessing children for only learning disabilities and learning disorders without looking for other comorbid conditions is problematic. The most important advances in pediatric psychiatry have been the result of researchers carefully checking children for all possible conditions.

Of particular importance is the comorbid occurrence of attention deficit hyperactivity disorder (ADHD) and learning disorders. Learning disabilities and ADHD often occur in combination (Deutsch-Smith, 2004). If a student has a learning disorder, that child has a 20–40 percent chance of having ADHD. That is about a five times increase over the general population. Some studies have even shown that 70 percent of children with ADHD also have a learning disability (Mayes, Calhoun, & Cromwell, 2000).

"Discrepancy" in Diagnosing a Learning Disability

According to Ortiz (2004), "Perhaps the most controversial aspect of the definition of LD is that the observed academic problems are greater than what might be expected based on the child's intellectual ability." This assumption is rarely questioned because it seems to make the most sense. As noted previously, LD is generally not diagnosed in individuals who have mental retardation, because it is expected that people with low cognitive ability will have problems learning to read, write, or do math. On the other hand, an assumption implicit in most definitions of LD is that a child would be able to perform at a level consistent with ability level were it not for the presence of LD. That is, children with LD are performing below their ability, intelligence, or potential.

Under the provisions of IDEA, decisions regarding the presence or absence of any disability, as well as the provision of special education services, are determined by a multidisciplinary team, which, by law, must include the parents, a regular education teacher, an administrator, and all professional staff who have evaluated the child. The notion of *discrepancy* is reflected in IDEA, which states that "a team may determine that a child has a specific learning disability" if two conditions are met: (1) the child does not achieve commensurate with his or her age and ability levels if provided with learning experiences appropriate for the child's age and ability levels and (2) the team finds that a child has a *severe discrepancy* between achievement and intellectual ability.

There are numerous criticisms of using discrepancy formulas, including the following:

- IQ tests are not reliable and are unfair to many groups of children.
- Results have little utility in planning a student's educational program.
- The process is not helpful in determining which interventions might be successful.
- The outcomes are not related to performance in the classroom, in the general education curriculum, or on district- or statewide assessments.
- Children must fail before they qualify for needed services (Smith, Pollaway, Patton, & Dowdy, 2004, p. 114).

The Exclusionary Clause

The definition of *learning disability* under IDEA also has what is referred to as an "exclusionary clause." The exclusionary clause states that a learning disability "does not include a learning problem that is primarily the result of visual, hearing or motor disabilities, of mental retardation, of emotional disturbance, or of environmental, cultural, or economic disadvantage" (34 C.F.R § 300.7[c][10]). The purpose of this exclusionary clause is to help prevent the improper labeling of children, especially those from distinct cultures who have acquired learning styles, language, or behaviors that are not compatible with the academic requirements of schools in dominant culture. However, the exclusionary clause has generated tremendous debate and controversy among experts in the field.

The wording of the "exclusion clause" in the federal definition of *learning disabilities* lends itself to the misinterpretation that individuals with learning disabilities cannot be multihandicapped or be from different cultural and linguistic backgrounds. It is essential to understand and recognize the learning disabilities as they might occur within the varying disability categories as well as different cultural and linguistic groups. Individuals within these groups frequently have received inappropriate educational assessment, planning, and instruction because they could not be identified as learning disabled.

Characteristics of Specific Learning Disabilities

No one sign shows a person has a learning disability. However, "unexpected underachievement" is the defining characteristic of learning disabilities (Deutsch-Smith, 2004; Friend, 2005; Gargiulo, 2004; Hallahan & Kauffman, 2006; Vaughn, Elbaum, & Boardman, 2001). Experts look for a noticeable difference between how well children do in school and how well they could do, given their intelligence or ability.

A child with a learning disability may exhibit the following characteristics:

- Cognitive difficulties:
  - Poor selective attention (Zera & Lucian, 2001)
  - Inattention or difficulty focusing on the task
  - Problems with memory, whether short-term, long-term, or both (Swanson, 2000)
  - Perceptual problems (Lerner, 2002; Smith, 1998)
- Academic difficulties:
  - Difficulty with oral fluency (Mercer, Campbell, Miller, Mercer, & Lane, 2000)
  - Making many mistakes when reading aloud, and repeating and pausing often
  - Very messy handwriting or holding a pencil awkwardly
  - Difficulty processing information (Geary, Hamson, & Hoard, 1999)
  - Learning language late and having a limited vocabulary
  - Trouble remembering the sounds that letters make or hearing slight differences between words

- o Difficulties in written language (Roth, 2000; Wong, 2000)
- o Mispronouncing words or using a wrong word that sounds similar
- o Trouble organizing what he wants to say or not being able to think of the word he needs for writing or conversation
- o Making many mistakes when reading aloud and repeating and pausing often
- o Very messy handwriting or holding a pencil awkwardly
- o Difficulties in reading (Bell, McCallum, & Cox, 2003)
- o Difficulties in mathematics (Mazzocco, 2001; Witzel, Smith, & Brownell, 2001)
- o Trouble learning the alphabet, rhyming words, or connecting letters to their sounds
- o Confusing math symbols and misreading numbers
- o Not being able to retell a story in order (what happened first, second, third)
- o Not knowing where to begin a task or how to go on from there
- Social and emotional difficulties:
  - o Deficits in social skills (Kavale & Forness, 1996)
  - o Rejection by peers and classmates (Pavri & Luftig, 2000)
  - o Difficulties making and keeping friends (Pavri & Monda-Amaya, 2001)
  - o Feeling lonely and isolated in adolescence (Tur-Kaspa, Weisel, & Segev, 1998)
  - o Poor social skills (Gresham, Sugai, & Horner, 2001)
  - o Not following the social rules of conversation, such as taking turns, and perhaps standing too close to the listener
- Behavioral difficulties:
  - o Difficulties communicating with others, leading to inappropriate behaviors (Vallace, Cummings, & Humphries, 1998)
  - o Trouble understanding jokes, comic strips, and sarcasm
  - o Trouble following directions

Characteristics of children with learning disabilities will be addressed in much more detail in Chapter 2.

Educational Implications of Specific Learning Disabilities

Learning disabilities tend to be diagnosed when children reach school age (National Dissemination Center for Children with Disabilities, 2004).

This is because school focuses on the very things that may be difficult for the child—reading, writing, and math, as well as listening, speaking, and reasoning. Teachers and parents notice that the child is not learning as expected. These students' low achievement separates them more each school year from their classmates without disabilities (Deshler et al., 2001).

With effective instruction, children with LD can learn more easily and successfully. For school-aged children (including preschoolers), special education and related services are important sources of help. Over 30 years of research findings about learning disabilities and the affected students have shown that intervention using validated and best practices make a positive difference in these students' performance (Hallahan & Kauffman, 2006; Swanson & Sachse-Lee, 2000).

2

Characteristics
of Children With
Learning Disabilities

Children with learning disabilities are a heterogeneous group. These children are a diverse group of individuals, exhibiting potential difficulties in many different areas. For example, one child with a learning disability may experience significant reading problems, while another may experience no reading problems whatsoever but have significant difficulties with written expression.

Various learning disabilities may be mild, moderate, or severe. Students differ, too, in their coping skills. According to Bowe (2005),

> Some learn to adjust to LD so well that they "pass" as not having a disability while others struggle throughout their lives to even do "simple" things. Despite these differences, LD always begins in childhood and is always is a life-long condition. (p. 71)

Over the years, parents, educators, and other professionals have identified a wide variety of characteristics associated with learning disabilities (Gargiulo, 2004). One of the earliest profiles, developed by Clements (1966), includes the following ten frequently cited attributes:

1. Hyperactivity

2. Perceptual-motor impairments

3. Emotional labiality

4. Coordination problems

5. Disorders of attention

6. Impulsivity

7. Disorders of memory and thinking

8. Academic difficulties

9. Language deficits

10. Equivocal neurological signs

Almost 35 years later, Lerner (2000) identified eight learning and behavioral characteristics of individuals with learning disabilities:

- Disorders of attention
- Poor motor abilities
- Psychological process deficits and information processing problems
- Oral language difficulties
- Reading difficulties
- Written language difficulties
- Quantitative disorders
- Social skills deficits

According to Gargiulo (2004), not all students with learning disabilities will exhibit these characteristics, while many pupils who demonstrate these behaviors are quite successful in the classroom. As Smith (1979) observes, it is the quantity, intensity, and duration of the behaviors that lead to the problems in school and elsewhere.

The focus of this chapter will be to discuss the most commonly seen characteristics of children with learning disabilities. In almost all cases, a single student will not have deficits in all areas. Understanding the characteristics of children with learning disabilities is absolutely essential as a future educator in developing prereferral interventions, in making appropriate referrals, and in identifying effective adaptations and intervention strategies (Smith et al., 2004).

Academic Achievement Deficits

Children with learning disabilities often struggle with various areas of academic performance. During the elementary school years, a discrepancy between ability and achievement begins to emerge. Often puzzling to teachers, these students seem to have strengths similar to their peers in several areas, but their rate of learning is unexpectedly slower (Smith et al., 2004). These problems usually persist from the primary grades through the end of formal schooling, including college (Bradshaw, 2001; Gregg, Coleman, Stennett, & Davis, 2002).

Academic deficits for children with learning disabilities normally fall into the following areas:

- Reading
- Mathematics
- Written expression

Some children have problems in only one academic area, while others may experience difficulties in all three.

Reading

Reading provides a fundamental way for individuals to exchange information. It is also a means by which much of the information presented in school is learned. As a result, reading is the academic area most often associated with academic failure. Reading is a complex process that requires numerous skills for its mastery. Consequently, identifying the skills that lead to success in reading is extremely important.

Reading difficulties are observed among students with learning disabilities more than challenges in any other area of academic performance. It is estimated that as many as 90 percent of students with learning disabilities have reading difficulties, and even the low estimates are approximately 60 percent (Bender, 2001). Most authorities believe that this problem is related to deficient language skills, especially phonological awareness—that is, the ability to understand that speech flow can be broken into smaller sound units, such as words, syllables, and phonemes.

According to Hallahan and Kauffman (2003), it is easy to see why problems with phonology would be at the heart of many reading difficulties. If people have problems breaking words into their component sounds, they will have trouble learning to read. And there is suggestive evidence that readers of English are more susceptible than readers of some other languages to problems with phonological awareness. Some have speculated that this is why reading disabilities are more prevalent in English-speaking countries than in some other countries (Hallahan & Kauffman, p.162).

Becoming a skilled reader is so important in our culture that an unskilled reader is at a great disadvantage in school and in the workplace. The following problems may prevent a child with learning disabilities from learning to read (Kirk, Gallagher, & Anastasiow, 2003, p. 224):

- Faulty auditory perception without hearing impairment
- Slow auditory or visual processing
- Inability to distinguish or separate the sounds of spoken words
- Lack of knowledge of the purpose of reading
- Failure to attend to critical aspects of the word, sentence, or paragraph
- Failure to understand that letters represent units of speech

Recent research has begun to reveal a great deal about the fundamental nature of children's reading disabilities and the type of instruction most likely to remediate reading problems (Jenkins & O'Conner, 2001). In summarizing the research, Torgeson and Wagner (1998) state that (1) the most severe reading problems of children with learning disabilities lie at the word, rather than the text, level of processing (i.e., inability to accurately and fluently decode single words) and (2) the most common cognitive limitation of these children involves a dysfunction in the awareness of the phonological structure of words in oral language (p. 226).

Clearly, problems with reading process are very prevalent among students identified as having learning disabilities. However, the specific problems that they have in reading vary as much as the many components of the reading process (Hardman, Drew, & Egan, 2005). These difficulties include, but are not limited to, the following:

- Oral reading
- Reading comprehension
- Word recognition skills
- Reading habits

Oral Reading

Many students with learning disabilities have difficulties with reading fluency (Mercer et al., 2000). Reading fluency, most frequently defined as the rate of accurate reading (correct words per minute), is more than a status symbol for children; it is an important indicator of reading ability (Hunt & Marshall, 2005). Students with learning disabilities may read aloud in a word-by-word manner without appropriate inflection or rhythm, unable to relate the patterns of spoken language to the printed word. Students with a weakness in this area often dread being asked to read aloud in class (Friend, 2005).

According to Salvia and Ysseldyke (1998), common oral reading problems include the following:

- *Omissions:* The student skips individual words or groups of words.
- *Insertion:* The student inserts one or more words into the sentence.
- *Substitution:* The student replaces one or more words in the passage with one or more meaningful words.
- *Gross mispronunciation of a word:* The student's pronunciation of a word bears little resemblance to the proper pronunciation.
- *Hesitation:* The student hesitates for two or more seconds before pronouncing a word.
- *Inversion:* The student changes the order of words appearing in a sentence.
- *Disregard of punctuation:* The student fails to observe punctuation; for example, the student may not pause for a comma or stop for a period or indicate a vocal inflection, a question mark, or an exclamation point.

Analyzing Oral Reading Miscues

An oral reading error is often referred to as a "miscue." A miscue is the difference between what a reader states is on a page and what is actually on the page. According to Vacca, Vacca, and Grove (1986), differences between what the reader says and what is printed on the page are not the result of random errors. Instead, these differences are "cued" by the thought and language of the reader, who is attempting to construct what the author is saying. Analysis of miscues can be of two types:

1. *Quantitative miscues:* With this type of miscue, the number of reading errors made by the student is counted.

2. *Qualitative miscues:* With this type of miscue, the focus is on the quality of the errors rather than the number of mistakes. The miscue is not based on problems related to word identification but rather on the differences between the miscues and the words on the pages. Consequently, some miscues are more significant than others (Vacca et al., 1986).

According to John (1985), a miscue is significant if it affects meaning. Miscues are generally significant when

- the meaning of the sentence or passages is significantly changed or altered, and the student does not correct the miscue;
- a nonword is used in place of the word in the passage;
- only a partial word is substituted for the word or phrase in the passage; or
- a word must be pronounced for the student.

Miscues are generally not significant when

- the meaning of the sentence or passage undergoes no change or only minimal change;
- they are self-corrected by the student;
- they are acceptable in the student's dialect; or
- they are later read correctly in the same passage.

Through miscue analysis, teachers can determine the extent to which the reader uses and coordinates graphic, sound, syntactic, and semantic information from the text. According to Goodman and Burke (1972), to analyze miscues, you should ask at least four crucial questions:

1. *Does the miscue change meaning?* If it does not, then it is semantically acceptable within the context of the sentence or passage.

2. *Does the miscue sound like language?* If it does, then it is grammatically acceptable within the context. Miscues are grammatically acceptable if they sound like language and serve as the same parts of speech as the text words.

3. *Do the miscue and the text word look and sound alike?* Substitution and mispronunciation miscues should be analyzed to determine how similar they are in approximating the graphic and pronunciation features of the text words.

4. *Was an attempt made to self-correct the miscue?* Self-corrections are revealing, because they demonstrate that the reader is attending to meaning and is aware that the initial miscuing did not make sense.

Oral reading problems often cause tremendous embarrassment for children. Children with oral reading problems may read in a strained voice with poor phrasing, ignoring punctuation and groping for words as would a much younger child. Polloway, Patton, and Serna (2001) confirm that a student's self-image and feelings of confidence are greatly affected by his or her reading experience. Deficits in reading skills can also lead to acting-out behavior and poor motivation.

Reading Comprehension

Students with learning disabilities often have difficulties with reading comprehension (Gersten, Williams, Fuchs, & Baker, 1998). These children often lack the skills required for understanding text and have poor word-analysis skills (Hunt & Marshall, 2005). Reading comprehension refers to a student's ability to understand what he or she is reading. Some students with reading comprehension difficulties are able to read a passage so fluently that you might assume they were highly proficient readers. However, when they are asked questions about what they have read, they show little or no understanding of the words. Students with this problem sometimes are referred to as "word callers" (Friend, 2005).

It is always necessary to assess not only decoding but also the ability to understand what is being decoded. According to Salvia and Ysseldyke (1998), there are six different types of reading comprehension skills:

1. *Literal comprehension:* The student reads the paragraph or story and is then asked questions based on it.

2. *Inferential comprehension:* The student reads a paragraph or story and must interpret what has been read.

3. *Listening comprehension:* The student is read a paragraph or story by the examiner and is then asked questions about what the examiner has read.

4. *Critical comprehension:* The student reads a paragraph or story and then analyzes, evaluates, or makes judgments about what has been read.

5. *Affective comprehension:* The student reads a paragraph or story, and the examiner evaluates the child's emotional responses to the text.

6. *Lexical comprehension:* The student reads a paragraph or story, and the examiner assesses the child's knowledge of vocabulary words.

Commonly seen reading comprehension problems of children with learning disabilities include the following:

- Difficulties recalling basic facts, resulting in being unable to answer specific questions about a passage (What was the dog's name in the story?)
- Difficulties recalling sequence, resulting in being unable to relate the sequence of the story that was read
- Difficulties recalling the main theme, resulting in being unable to recall the main topic of the story

Furthermore, when evaluating the reading behavior of a child on reading comprehension, it is important to ask the following questions:

- Does the student *guess* at answers to the questions presented?
- Does the student *show unwillingness to read* or to make attempts at reading?
- Does the student *skip* unknown words?
- Does the student *disregard* punctuation?
- Does the student *exhibit inattention* to the story line?
- Does the student *drop the tone of his or her voice* at the end of sentences?
- Does the student *display problems with sounding out* word parts and blends?
- Does the student *exhibit a negative attitude* toward reading?
- Does the student *express difficulty attacking* unknown words?

Word Recognition Skills

Students with learning disabilities often have difficulties with word recognition. Word recognition explores the student's ability with respect to sight vocabulary. According to Salvia and Ysseldyke (1998),

> A student learns the correct pronunciation of letters and words through a variety of experiences. The more exposure a student has to specific words and the more familiar those words become, the more readily he or she recognizes those words and is able to pronounce them correctly. (p. 464)

To identify written words, we use a number of different skills. Some of the most important word analysis skills include the following:

- The ability to associate sounds with the various letters and letter combinations used to write them (phonic analysis)
- Immediately recognizing and remembering words (sight-word reading)
- Using the surrounding text to help figure out a specific word

The above skills rely heavily on perception, selective attention, memory, and metacognitive skills. Thus, word recognition depends almost entirely on the cognitive skills that are most problematic for individuals with disabilities (Hunt & Marshall, 2005).

Common word recognition errors include the following (Gargiulo, 2004):

- *Omissions:* Omitting a word (Tom saw [a] cat.)
- *Insertions:* Inserting words (The dog ran [fast] after the cat.)
- *Substitutions:* Reversing letters in a word (*no* for *on*; *was* for *saw*)
- *Mispronunciations:* (*mister* for *miser*)

- *Transpositions:* Reading words in the wrong order (She away ran, instead of, She ran away.)
- *Unknown words:* Hesitating for five seconds at words the individual cannot pronounce
- *Slow, choppy reading:* Not recognizing words quickly enough (20 to 30 words per minute)

Reading Habits

Children with reading difficulties often have poor reading habits. As a teacher, it is critical that you be aware of these habits when watching your students read on a daily basis. Some of the behaviors that are exhibited by children with poor reading habits include the following (Gargiulo, 2004):

- Tension movements (frowning, fidgeting, using a high-pitched tone of voice)
- Insecurity (refusing to read, crying, attempting to distract the teacher)
- Loses place (losing place frequently)
- Lateral head movements (jerking head)
- Holds material close (deviating extremely from 15 to 18 inches)

Math

Although disorders of reading have traditionally received more emphasis than problems with mathematics, the latter are now gaining a great deal of attention (Hunt & Marshall, 2005). Authorities now recognize that math difficulties are second only to reading disabilities as an academic problem area for students with learning disabilities (Hallahan & Kauffman, 2003). Researchers estimate that about one out of every four pupils with learning disabilities receives assistance because of difficulties with mathematics (Rivera, 1997). According to Lerner (2002), each student with mathematical difficulties is unique; not all children exhibit the same deficiency or impairment.

Students with learning disabilities may have problems with both math calculations and math reasoning (U.S. Office of Education, 1977). These students often have a number of problems in mathematical thinking (Hunt & Marshall, 2005). Mathematical thinking is a process that begins early in most children. Even before formal education begins, children are exposed to various situations that involve the application of mathematical concepts. As they enter formal schooling, they take the knowledge of what they previously learned and begin to apply it in a more formal manner.

It is necessary to understand that *mathematics* and *arithmetic* are actually two different terms. Although most people use them interchangeably, they each have distinct meanings. According to *Merriam-Webster's Collegiate Dictionary* (2006), arithmetic is

> **1 a :** a branch of mathematics that deals usu[ally] with the non-negative real numbers including sometimes the transfinite cardinals and with the application of the operations of addition, subtraction, multiplication, and division to them

while mathematics is

> **1 :** the science of numbers and their operations, interrelations, combinations, generalizations, and abstractions and of space, configurations and their structure, measurement, transformations, and generalizations

Mathematics involves many different abilities:

- Solving problems
- Recognizing how to interpret results
- Applying mathematics in practical situations
- Using mathematics for prediction
- Estimating
- Doing computational skills
- Understanding measurement
- Creating and reading graphs and charts

Schools begin the process of learning math skills in kindergarten and proceed throughout the child's formal education. Even at the college level, mathematics is often a core requirement in many liberal arts schools. In general, next to reading, mathematics is probably the area most frequently assessed in school systems.

Analysis and Interpretation of Math Skills

According to McLoughlin and Lewis (1990), mathematics is one of the school subjects best suited for error analysis because students respond in writing on most tasks, thereby producing a permanent record of their work. Also, there is usually only one correct answer to mathematics questions and problems, and scoring is unambiguous.

Today, the most common use of error analysis in mathematics is assessment of computation skills. Cox (1975) differentiates between systematic computation errors and errors that are random or careless mistakes. With systematic errors, students are consistent in their use of an incorrect number fact, operation, or algorithm.

McLoughlin and Lewis (1990) identified four error types in computational analysis:

1. *Incorrect operation:* The student selects the incorrect operation. For example, the problem requires subtraction, but the student adds.

2. *Incorrect number fact:* The number fact recalled by the student is inaccurate. For example, the student recalls the product of 9×6 as 52.

3. *Incorrect algorithm:* The procedures used by the student to solve the problem are inappropriate. The student may skip a step, apply the correct steps in the wrong sequence, or use an inaccurate method.

4. *Random error:* The student's response is incorrect and apparently random. For example, the student writes 100 as the answer to 42×6 (p. 354).

Different types of errors can occur in the mathematics process other than the four mentioned above.

Arithmetic Operations

For example, a student may make a mistake or error in applying the appropriate arithmetic operations (e.g., $50 - 12 = 62$). Here, the student used the operation of addition rather than subtraction. The student may understand how to do both operations but consistently get these types of questions wrong on tests by using the wrong operation.

Slips

Another problem that the student may encounter is a "slip." When a slip occurs, it is more likely due to a simple mistake rather than a pattern of problems. For example, if a child correctly subtracts 5 from 20 in eight problems but for some reason not in the ninth problem, the error is probably due to a simple slip rather than a serious operational or processing problem. One error on one problem is not an error pattern. Error patterns can be assessed by analyzing all correct and incorrect answers. When designing a program plan for a particular child in mathematics, it is critical to establish not only the nature of the problems but also the patterns of problems that occur in the child's responses.

Handwriting

Also, handwriting can play an important role in mathematics. Scoring a math test often involves reading numbers written down on an answer sheet. If a student's handwriting is difficult or impossible to interpret, the evaluator can have serious problems obtaining valid scores. When a student's handwriting is not clear on a math test, it is important that the evaluator ask the student to help read the answers. By doing so, the evaluator is analyzing the math skills that need to be assessed rather than trying to decode the student's responses.

Written Expression

Many individuals with learning disabilities exhibit deficits in written language (Hallahan, Kauffman, & Lloyd, 1999). Learning disabilities in the area of written expression are beginning to receive more recognition as a serious problem (Smith et al., 2004).

Writing is a highly complex method of expression involving the integration of eye-hand, linguistic, and conceptual abilities. As a result, it is usually the last skill children master. Whereas reading is usually considered the receptive form of a graphic symbol system, writing is considered the expressive form of that system. The primary concern in the assessment of composition skills is the content of the student's writing, not its form.

The term *written language* refers to a variety of interrelated graphic skills, including the following:

- *Composition:* The ability to generate ideas and to express them in an acceptable grammar, while adhering to certain stylistic conventions
- *Spelling:* The ability to use letters to construct words in accordance with accepted usage
- *Handwriting:* The ability to execute physically the graphic marks necessary to produce legible compositions or messages (Hallahan et al., 1999)

The impact of written language problems increases with a student's age because so many school assignments require a written product. Students with written language problems often

- feel overwhelmed by the idea of getting started;
- struggle to organize and use the mechanics of writing;
- struggle to develop their fluency;

- have difficulties spelling and constructing written products in a legible fashion; and
- submit written work that is too brief.

Many students with difficulties with written language use a "retrieve-and-write" approach, in which they retrieve from immediate memory "whatever seems appropriate and write it down." They seldom use the self-regulation and self-assessment strategies of competent writers: setting a goal or plan to guide their writing, organizing their ideas, drafting, self-assessing, and rewriting. As a result, they produce poorly organized compositions containing a few poorly developed ideas (Sexton, Harris, & Graham, 1998, cited in Heward, 2005).

Handwriting

Handwriting refers to the actual motor activity that is involved in writing. Most students are taught manuscript (printing) initially and then move to cursive writing (script) in later grades. Some educators advocate that only manuscript or only cursive should be taught. In truth, problems may appear among students in either system.

Children's writing changes as they mature. The focus of a youngster's writing shifts from (1) the process of writing (handwriting and spelling) to (2) the written product (having written something) to (3) communication with readers (getting across one's message, Hallahan et al., 1999, p. 396).

Gargiulo (2004) notes that early on, pupils focus on becoming competent in mastering the mechanical aspects of composition-spelling and handwriting; in the later grades, they learn to organize and present their ideas in a lucid and logical fashion. Children with learning disabilities, however, lag behind their nondisabled peers. Investigators have observed that individuals with learning disabilities use less complex sentence structures, incorporate fewer ideas, produce poorly organized paragraphs, and write less complex stories (Gargiulo, p. 219).

Spelling

Spelling is the ability to use letters to construct words in accordance with accepted usage. Spelling ability is viewed by some teachers and school administrators as equally important as other academic skills. Being a poor speller does not necessarily mean that a child has a learning disorder. However, when poor spelling occurs with poor reading and/or arithmetic, then there is reason for concern. It appears that many of the learning skills required for good spelling are the same ones that enable students to become good readers.

Learning to spell is a developmental process, and young children go through a number of stages as they begin to acquire written language skills. Writing begins in the preschool years as young children observe and begin to imitate the act of writing.

Hunt and Marshall (2005) note that many students with learning disabilities spell words as if approaching them for the first time, without reference to an image of the word held in memory. The difficulties that students with learning disabilities have in learning and applying the rules of phonics, visualizing the word correctly, and evaluating spellings result in frequent misspellings, even as they become more adept at reading. It is not uncommon to find the same word spelled five or six different ways on the same paper, regardless of whether the student is in the fifth grade or college (e.g., *ther, there, thare,* and *they're* for *their*).

Moats (1994) suggests that prior research has shown spelling to be a complex process that is not simply mechanical. A sign that a child may have a learning disability, not just a learning problem, is the ability to read well coupled with poor spelling ability. Spelling may be the most obvious performance deficit for children with a learning disability (Kirk et al., 2003).

Analysis of Spelling Skills

Several questions should be addressed before one begins to analyze a child's spelling abilities:

Does the child have sufficient mental ability to learn to spell?

This information can be obtained from the school psychologist if an intellectual evaluation was administered. However, if no such test was administered, then a group school abilities index may be present in the child's permanent folder.

Are the child's hearing, speech, and vision adequate?

This information can be obtained through the permanent record folder, information in the nurse's office, or informal screening procedures.

What is the child's general level of spelling ability according to teacher comments, past evaluations, or standardized tests?

Teacher comments and observations about the child's spelling history are very important to show patterns of disability. Also, look at standardized tests to see if patterns exist through the years on such tests.

It is also important to look at the following:

- The child's attitude toward spelling in the classroom
- The extent to which the child relies on a dictionary in the classroom
- The extent of spelling errors in classroom written work
- Any patterns of procrastination or avoidance of written work
- The student's study habits and methods of work in the classroom
- The history of scores on classroom spelling tests
- Any observable handwriting difficulties
- Any evidence of fatigue as a factor in the child's spelling performance

Spelling Errors Primarily Due to Auditory or Visual Channel Deficits

Certain spelling errors may be evident in students with certain auditory channel deficits:

- *Auditory discrimination problems or cultural problems:* The child substitutes *t* for *d* or *sh* for *ch*.
- *Auditory discrimination problems:* The child confuses vowels, for example, spells *bit* as *bet*.
- *Auditory acuity or discrimination problems:* The child does not hear subtle differences in, nor discriminate between, sounds and often leaves vowels out of two-syllable words.
- *Auditory-visual association:* The child uses a synonym, such as *house* for *home*.
- *Auditory-visual associative memory:* The child takes wild guesses with little or no relationship between the letters or words used and the spelling words dictated, such as spelling *dog* for *home* or writing *phe* for *home*.

Certain spelling errors may be evident in students with certain visual channel deficits:

- *Visual memory problems:* The child visualizes the beginning or the ending of words but omits the middle of the words (spells *hppy* for *happy*).
- *Visual memory sequence:* The child gives the correct letters but in the wrong sequence (writes the word *the* as *teh* or *hte*).
- *Visual discrimination problems:* The child inverts letters (writing *u* for *n* or *m* for *w*).
- *Visual memory:* The child spells words phonetically that are nonphonetic in configuration (*tuff* for *tough*).

In general, common spelling errors to look for in students with dysorthographia include the addition of unneeded letters, reversal of vowels, reversal of syllables, and the phonemic spelling of nonphonemic words.

Fortunately, the writing and spelling skills of most students with learning disabilities can be improved through strategy instruction, frequent opportunities to practice writing, and systematic feedback (Heward, 2005).

Language Deficits

Students with learning disabilities often have difficulties with the mechanical and social uses of language (Hallahan & Kauffman, 2006). Specific mechanical deficits difficulties are often present in the three areas (Gargiulo, 2004):

1. *Syntax:* Rule systems that determine how words are organized into sentences

2. *Semantics:* Word meanings

3. *Phonology:* The study of how individual sounds make up words

Language deficits are found in the areas of oral expression and listening comprehension. These two areas control our ability to communicate with others, so a deficit in either or both can have a major impact on the quality of life of a child, as well as his or her life in education (Smith et al., 2004). Studies have found that more than 60 percent of students with learning disabilities have some type of language disorder (Bryan, Bay, Lopez-Reyna, & Donahue, 1991).

Oral Language Problems

Students with LD frequently experience difficulties with oral expression—a problem that can affect both academic and social interactions. Common oral language problems include the following:

- *Choosing the appropriate word:* Children with LD will often use a less appropriate word because the right word will not come to them.
- *Understanding complex sentence structures*
- *Responding to questions*
- *Difficulties in retrieving words:* The response rate of children with learning disabilities may be slower than that of their nondisabled peers, and they may speak more slowly.

In sum, children with LD tend to use simpler, less mature language and confuse sequences in retelling a story. These deficits in expressive language suggest possible deficits in receptive language or listening, as well (Smith, 1994, cited in Smith et al., 2004).

Listening Comprehension Problems

Listening problems can also be misinterpreted. A child with a disability in listening demonstrates that disability in a negative way, for example, by failing to follow directions or by appearing oppositional or unmotivated. A teacher's careful observation and assessment of a student's language ability is important for ensuring the student's success (Smith et al., 2004).

Problems With Pragmatics

One aspect of oral expression that is receiving increased attention is pragmatics—the functional use of language in social situations. Researchers note that children with learning disabilities sometimes experience communication problems in social settings (Bryan, 1997). Research in the field of children with language-learning disabilities has begun to focus more and more on the area of pragmatics. Students with LD may do the following:

- Need extra time to process incoming information
- Not understand the meaning of the words or sequences
- Miss nonverbal language cues
- Not understand jokes
- Laugh inappropriately or at the wrong times
- Have difficulty doing group work
- Have difficulty giving or following directions
- Have conversations marked by long silences
- Not be skilled in responding to statements
- Not be skilled in responding to questions
- Have a tendency to answer their questions
- Make those with whom they talk uncomfortable (Hallahan & Kauffman, 2003)

Participating in conversations with friends can be especially troublesome for someone with a learning disability. The ebb and flow that is characteristic of conversations may elude them, and nonverbal language clues may also be overlooked. In short, many individuals with learning disabilities are not good conversationalists (Gargiulo, 2004). The have great difficulty trying to engage in the mutual give-and-take that conversation between two people requires.

Disorders of Attention

Attention is a critical skill in learning. Conte (1991) suggests that to be effective learners, children must be able to initiate attention, direct their attention appropriately, sustain their attention according to the task demands, and shift attention when appropriate. Deficits in these areas can have an impact on all areas of school. When children are not paying attention, they cannot respond appropriately to questions, follow directions, or take notes during a lecture. Social problems occur when the student interrupts others and does not listen to peers. Estimates of the number of students with learning disabilities who have attention problems range from 41 to 80 percent (Long, 1995, cited in Smith et al., 2004).

Attention problems for children with learning disabilities are often characterized as "short attention spans." A short attention span is defined as an inability to focus one's attention on a task for more than a few seconds or minutes. Parents and teachers note that children with LD do the following:

- Cannot sustain attention for more than a short time
- Exhibit excessive daydreaming
- Are highly distractible

Individuals with learning disabilities often have attention problems (Forness & Kavale, 2001). Their attention difficulties are often severe enough to be diagnosed as also having attention deficit hyperactivity disorder (ADHD). ADHD is a diagnosis normally made by either a psychiatrist or psychologist, using the criteria as established by the American Psychiatric Association in the *Diagnostic and Statistical Manual of Mental Disorders* (1994). Although estimates vary, researchers have consistently found an overlap of 10 to 25 percent between ADHD and learning disabilities (Forness & Kavale, 2002).

Several characteristics of ADHD have long been recognized in many children with learning disabilities, and there is a significant level of comorbidity (a situation in which multiple conditions occur together) between the two conditions (some estimates as high as 25 percent).

Achievement Discrepancy

Although students who receive special education services under the learning disabilities category are an extremely heterogeneous group, it is important to remember that the fundamental defining characteristic of students with learning disabilities is specific and significant achievement deficits in the presence of adequate overall intelligence (Heward, 2005). Students with LD perform below expectations based on their measured potential in addition to scoring below their peers in overall achievement. Attempts to quantify the discrepancy between academic achievement and academic potential for students with LD have appeared in the literature for some time, but the field still lacks a broadly accepted explanation of the phenomenon (Roderiques, 2002, cited in Hardman et al., 2005).

Early in the school years, youngsters with LD may find themselves two to four years behind their peers in level of academic achievement, and many fall even further behind as they continue in the educational system. This discouraging pattern often results in students dropping out of high school or graduating without proficiency in basic reading, writing, or math skills (U.S. Department of Education, 2002, cited in Hardman et al., 2005, p.178).

The difficulties experienced by children with learning disabilities—especially for those who cannot read at grade level—are substantial and pervasive and usually last throughout their lives (Mercer, 1997). The tendency to think of learning disabilities as "mild" disabilities erroneously supports "the notion that a learning disability is little more than a minor inconvenience rather than the serious, life-long condition it is and often detracts from the real needs of these students" (Hallahan, 1998, p. 4, cited in Heward, 2005).

Memory Deficits

It is well documented that children and adolescents with learning disabilities have significant difficulties remembering both academic information and nonacademic information, such as doctors' appointments, homework assignments, multiplication facts, directions, and telephone numbers. Both teachers and parents report that memory skills are inconsistent.

Parents often state that they cannot understand how their children can be so intelligent and forget such simple things. Early research in learning disabilities has documented students with learning disabilities as having a real deficit in memory (Hallahan & Kauffman, 2006). Teachers frequently comment that, with these students, it seems to be "in one ear and out the other," which can be highly aggravating for teachers as well as parents (Gargiulo, 2004). In many cases, these students seem to learn material one day but cannot recall it the next (Hardman et al., 2005). For example, a student may know the multiplication facts on Thursday but fail the test on Friday.

Several studies have suggested that students with learning disabilities have more deficits in memory than students without learning disabilities, except in the area of long-term memory (Swanson, 1994). Students with memory deficits have difficulty with the following tasks:

- Retaining learned information
- Repeating information read or heard
- Following multiple directions
- Performing tasks in the right sequence (Smith et al., 2004)

The memory difficulties faced by students with learning disabilities are normally either in short-term memory (STM) or working memory (WM). STM involves the ability to recall information after a short period of time. Short-term memory tasks involve the recall, in correct order, of either aurally or visually presented information (such as a list of digits, letters, or pictures) shortly after hearing or seeing the items several times (Hallahan et al., 1999). Working memory requires that the individual retain information while simultaneously engaging in another cognitive activity.

According to Silver (2001), people with LD are more likely to have concerns with short-term rather than long-term memory. He explained that children and youth with these limitations need to concentrate upon new information and repeat it continually to keep it in short-term memory. If their attention is disrupted, the information may be lost (Bowe, 2005).

Working memory is involved, for example, when we try to remember a person's address while also listening to directions on how to arrive there (Swanson, 1994). Deficits in memory, particularly working memory, often translate into difficulties in the classroom. Success with reading and math seems to depend more on working memory than short-term memory (Swanson). Working memory also appears to be crucial for word recognition and reading comprehension (Ashbaker & Swanson, 1996).

Although there are various theories as to why students with learning disabilities have difficulties with memory tasks, it appears that they do not use "strategies for remembering" the way their nondisabled peers do. For example, when presented with a list of words to memorize, most children will rehearse the names to themselves. They will make use of categories by rehearsing the words and grouping them together. Students with learning disabilities are not likely to use these names spontaneously (Hallahan & Kauffman, 2003).

O'Shaughenessy and Swanson (1998) suggest that the problem is mainly with an inability to code new information for memory storage and a decreased motivation for difficult mental effort. On a positive note, when children with learning disabilities are taught a memory strategy, they perform memory tasks as well as students without learning disabilities (Smith et al., 2004).

Cognitive Deficits

Students with learning disabilities often demonstrate problems in cognition. *Cognition* is a broad term covering many different aspects of thinking and problem solving. Students with learning disabilities often exhibit disorganized thinking that results in problems in planning and organizing their lives at home (Hallahan & Kauffman, 2003). Research suggests that children with LD have differing, rather than uniformly deficient, cognitive abilities (Henry, 2001). This finding has led to the development of specific, highly focused instruction for individuals with learning disabilities to replace generic curricula reflecting the assumption that their cognitive skills are generally poor (Hardman et al., 2005).

According to Smith et al. (2004), students with problems in cognition may have the following challenges:

- Make poor decisions
- Make frequent errors
- Have trouble getting started on a task
- Have delayed verbal responses
- Require more supervision
- Have trouble adjusting to change
- Have difficulties understanding social expectations
- Require concrete demonstrations
- Have trouble using previously learned information in a new situation

Metacognition Deficits

Students with learning disabilities often have problems with metacognition. *Metacognition* is defined as one's understanding of the strategies available for learning a task and the regulatory mechanisms needed to complete the task.

Metacognition has at least three components:

1. *Recognize task requirements:* Students with LD frequently have problems judging how difficult tasks can be. For example, they may approach the reading of highly technical information with the same level of intensity as reading for pleasure.

2. *Select and implement appropriate strategies:* Students with LD often do not come up with strategies to help themselves within and outside of school. For example, if asked to list ways in which they can help themselves remember to bring their homework to school the next day, they may not have any ideas, whereas nondisabled peers would tell you they could write a note to themselves, put the homework by the front door, etc.

3. *Monitor and adjust performance:* Students with LD often have problems with comprehension monitoring. *Comprehension monitoring* is the ability to keep track of one's own comprehension of reading material and to make adjustments to comprehend better while reading. For example, students with LD may not have a good sense that they do not understand what they are reading. Good readers, on the other hand, are often able to make necessary adjustments, such as slowing down and/or re-reading difficult passages. Students with reading problems are also likely to have problems picking out the main ideas of paragraphs.

Hallahan et al. (1999) refer to metacognition as "thinking about thinking." Students with problems in this area might have difficulty focusing on listening, purposefully remembering important information, connecting that information to prior knowledge, making sense out of the new information, and using what they know to solve a problem. They often lack strategies for planning and organizing, setting priorities, and predicting and solving problems. An important component of metacognition is the ability to evaluate one's own behavior and behave differently when identifying inappropriate behavior or mistakes (Smith et al., 2004). Competency as a learner requires that students exhibit these metacognitive skills (Kluwe, 1987).

Social-Emotional Problems

The literature suggests that to be socially accepted, students should be cooperative, share, offer pleasant greetings, have positive interactions with peers, ask for and give information, and make conversation (Gresham, 1982). Some children with LD have a real strength in the area of social skills. However, several characteristics of learning disabilities, like those noted concerning language, can create difficulties in social and emotional life (Smith et al., 2004).

Although not all children with LD have social-emotional problems, they do run a greater risk than their nondisabled peers of having such problems. In the early years, they are often rejected by their peers and have poor self-concepts (Sridhar & Vaughn, 2001). As adults, the scars from years of rejection can be painful and not easily forgotten (McGrady, Lerner, & Boscardin, 2001).

A possible reason for these social-emotional problems is that students with LD often have deficits in social cognition. They may have the following challenges:

- Misread social cues
- Misinterpret the feelings of others
- Not know when they are bothering others
- Be unaware of the effect of their behavior on someone else
- Be unable to take the perspective of others or put themselves in someone else's shoes

Research has consistently found a higher-than-normal rate of behavioral problems in the classroom among students with learning disabilities (Cullinan, 2002). In a study of 790 students enrolled in K–12 learning disabilities programs in Indiana, the percentage of students with behavioral problems (19 percent) remained consistent across grade levels. However, it should be noted that the relationships between students' behavioral problems and academic difficulties are not known. In other words, we do not know whether the academic deficits or the behavioral problems cause the other difficulty. Furthermore, many children with LD exhibit no behavioral problems at all (Heward, 2005).

Research further suggests that social interaction problems for students with LD seem to be more evident in those who have problems in the following areas:

- Math
- Visual-spatial tasks
- Tactual tasks, self-regulation
- Organization (Worling, Humphries, & Tannock, 1999)

After reviewing 152 different studies, Kavale and Forness (1996) concluded that 75 percent of students with learning disabilities exhibit deficits in social skills. Studies of teacher ratings also suggest that students with learning disabilities have lower social status than other students (Kavale & Forness). Research suggests that children with LD have social skills deficits, including the following:

- Being lower in social competency
- Feeling lower in school adjustment
- Feeling rejected by peers
- Having difficulty making friends
- Being seen by peers as overly dependent
- Being less likely to become leaders
- Resolving conflict
- Managing frustrations
- Initiating or joining a conversation or play activities
- Listening
- Demonstrating empathy
- Maintaining a friendship
- Working in groups

Some students with LD, however, experience no problems getting along with peers and teachers. For example, Sabornie and Kauffman (1986) reported no significant difference between the sociometric standing of 46 high school students with LD and that of 46 peers without disabilities. Moreover, they discovered that some of the students with LD enjoyed socially rewarding experiences in inclusive classrooms. One interpretation of these contradictory findings is that social competence and peer acceptance are not characteristics of LD but outcomes of the different social climates created by teachers, peers, parents, and others with whom students with LD interact (Vaughn, McIntosh, Schumm, Haager, & Callwood, 1993, cited in Heward, 2005).

In some cases, the social dimensions of life pose greater problems for students with learning disabilities than their specific academic deficits, yet this trait is essentially ignored in the definitions and labels related to learning disabilities. Many professionals would not support broadening the definition of learning disabilities to incorporate social and emotional dimensions, although it is clear that these are substantial (Hutchinson, Freeman, & Bell, 2002, cited in Hardman et al., 2005).

Years of failure can create other concerns. Wright-Strawderman and Watson (1992) found that 36 percent of a sample of students with learning disabilities indicated depression. Other researchers have reported psychological problems:

- Feelings of inadequacy
- Anxiety

- Frustration
- Anger (Bender, 2002)

Many students with LD are inept at understanding and interpreting social cues and social situations, which can easily lead to strained interpersonal relationships. Bryan (1997) suggests that the social-emotional difficulties of persons with learning disabilities may be the result of social imperceptiveness—a lack of skill in detecting subtle affective cues.

Nonverbal Learning Disorders (NLD)

Nonverbal learning disorders (NLD) is a neurological syndrome consisting of specific assets and deficits. The assets include early speech and vocabulary development, remarkable rote memory skills, attention to detail, early reading skills development, and excellent spelling skills. In addition, these individuals have the verbal ability to express themselves eloquently. Moreover, persons with NLD have strong auditory retention.

Four major categories of deficits and dysfunction also present themselves:

1. *Motoric:* Lack of coordination, severe balance problems, and difficulties with graphomotor skills

2. *Visual-spatial-organizational:* Lack of image, poor visual recall, faulty spatial perceptions, difficulties with executive functioning (the brain's ability to absorb information, interpret this information, and make decisions based upon this information), and problems with spatial relations

3. *Social:* Lack of ability to comprehend nonverbal communication, difficulties adjusting to transitions and novel situations, and deficits in social judgment and social interaction

4. *Sensory:* Sensitivity in any of the sensory modes: visual, auditory, tactile, taste, or olfactory

Foss (2001) reports that statements like the following are often true of individuals with a nonverbal learning disability:

- They talk a lot but really say very little.
- They see the "trees," not the "forest."
- They focus on details while not apprehending the main idea.
- They do not "read" facial expressions, gestures, or other nonverbal aspects of communication; they miss the subtleties and nuances.

- They may be inappropriate in their social interactions.
- They have few friends; friendships tend to be with older or younger persons rather than peers.
- They tend to process information in a linear, sequential fashion, not seeing multiple dimensions.

Motivational and Attribution Problems

Students with learning disabilities often lose the motivation to succeed in school. As failure starts to become more prominent, they begin to take on an external locus of control. *External locus of control* is a motivational term meaning that an individual believes that he or she is no longer in control over his or her fate in life. People with an external locus of control believe that they will have a good day or a bad day depending on how outside influences affect them. They feel powerless and no longer believe that they control their own destiny. On the other hand, those with an internal locus of control believe that they are "the captain of their own ships" and that they control their successes and failures. Students with an external locus of control believe that their lives are dictated by luck or fate rather than by internal factors, such as determination, hard work, or ability.

Chronic difficulties with academic assignments often lead children with learning disabilities to anticipate failure; success is seen as an unattainable goal no matter how hard they try. Seligman (1992) identifies this outlook as learned helplessness. Youngsters who maintain this attitude frequently give up and will not even attempt to complete the task. As a result, even when success is possible, the student no longer tries because of a mind-set that failure is inevitable anyway.

What individuals believe about what contributes to their own success or failure on a task is known as "attribution." Many students with learning disabilities attribute success, as well as failure, not to their own efforts but to situations or events beyond their control.

Because of their propensity for academic failure, individuals with learning disabilities tend to become passive or inactive learners. They are not actively involved or engaged in their own learning (Torgeson, 1977) and often fail to demonstrate initiative in the learning process. Swanson (1998) calls these pupils "actively inefficient learners."

Motivation is the desire to engage in an activity. Many special education and general education teachers, especially those in middle and high schools, comment that students with learning disabilities are not motivated to learn, and research suggests that this is a common characteristic of children with LD (Fulk, Brigham, & Lohman, 1998).

Perceptual Deficits

Many students with LD exhibit perceptual problems (Lerner, 2003). *Perception* does not pertain to whether a student sees or hears but rather to how that student's brain interprets what is seen or heard. Perceptual disorders affect the ability to recognize stimuli being received through sight, hearing, or touch and to discriminate between and interpret the sensations appropriately. A child with a learning disability might not have any problems in these areas, or the child might have deficits in any or all of them (Smith et al., 2004).

For example, a student with a visual perception problem may see perfectly well the letters *b-a-t* written on the page, but the student's brain interprets them as *t-a-b*. Problems in auditory perception often include difficulties with perceiving sounds that are not attributable to a hearing loss (Kruger, Kruger, Hugo, & Campbell, 2001). For example, some students may have trouble understanding whether the word spoken was *king* or *kin*, *hot* or *hut*, *fire* or *file*. The result can be misunderstood directions, poor communication, and awkwardness in social situations (Friend, 2005).

3

Types of Learning Disabilities

There are various types of learning disabilities. The focus of this chapter will be to address the most common types of learning disabilities, define them, discuss their characteristics, and draw some conclusions about each.

Auditory Processing Disorders

Auditory processing disorders (APD) interfere with an individual's ability to analyze or make sense of information taken in aurally (through the ears). This is different from problems involving hearing per se, such as deafness or being hard of hearing. Difficulties with auditory processing do not affect what is heard by the ear. The *disorder* part of auditory processing disorder means that something is adversely affecting the processing or interpretation of the information (National Institute on Deafness and Other Communication Disorders, 2004).

Diagnostic symptoms of individuals with auditory processing disorders include the following (Ciocci, 2002; Gertner, 2003):

- Difficulty with some or all listening activities
- Particular problems when activities occur in less-than-ideal listening environments

- Problems with sound discrimination
- Errors when speaking on a one-to-one basis, especially when there is competing background noise or speech
- Difficulty understanding information when speakers talk rapidly
- Difficulty understanding information when not devoting one's complete attention to the listening task
- Difficulty with unfamiliar discussion topics
- Difficulty performing or remembering several verbal tasks in a row
- Exhibiting weak phonemic systems (speech sound memories used in phonics, reading, and spelling)
- Often appearing as though not hearing well
- Frequently saying "What?" or "Huh?" in response to questions
- Not always being intimately in touch with the sounds in the environment, hence not always grasping exactly what has been said
- Having a history of middle ear infection
- Have lower academic performance
- Needing more time to process information
- Having difficulties with reading comprehension, vocabulary, and spelling
- Displaying behavior problems

An auditory processing disorder is a complex condition. It is sometimes misunderstood because many of the behaviors also appear in other conditions, such as attention deficit hyperactivity disorder (ADHD) and even depression. Symptoms of APD can range from mild to severe and can take many different forms. An auditory processing disorder does not interfere solely with speech and language; it can affect all areas of learning, especially reading and spelling. When instruction in school relies primarily on spoken language, the individual with an auditory processing disorder may have serious difficulty understanding the lesson or the directions (National Center for Learning Disabilities, 1999).

Dyscalculia (Arithmetic Disorders)

Dyscalculia is a term referring to a wide range of life-long learning disabilities involving math (National Center for Learning Disabilities, 2006). These disabilities affect a person's ability to understand and/or manipulate numbers, perform mathematical operations, and/or conceptualize numbers themselves as an abstract concept of comparative quantities.

Diagnostic symptoms of dyscalculia include difficulties with the following tasks (Learning Disabilities Association, 2005; Newman, 1998):

- Organizing problems on the page, keeping numbers lined up, following through on long division problems
- Putting language to math processes
- Understanding and doing word problems
- Keeping score or remembering how to keep score in games such as bowling
- Remembering dance step sequences or rules for playing sports
- Sight-reading music, learning fingering to play an instrument, etc.
- Abstract concepts of time and direction
- Grasping and remembering math concepts rules, formulas, and sequences (order of operations) and basic addition, subtraction, multiplication, and division facts
- Recalling schedules and sequences of past or future events
- Strategic planning for games such as chess
- Being on time
- Mentally figuring change due back or the amounts to pay for tips, taxes, etc.
- Maintaining a sense of direction
- Grasping concepts of formal music education
- Understanding money and cash transactions
- Athletic coordination (e.g., keeping up with rapidly changing physical directions as in aerobic, dance, and exercise classes)
- Recalling dates or addresses
- Visualizing or picturing the location of the numbers on the face of a clock or the geographical locations of states, countries, oceans, streets, etc.
- Long-term memory (retention and retrieval) of concepts (e.g., being able to perform math operations one day but drawing a blank the next)
- Retaining a memory of the "layout" of things (e.g., getting lost or disoriented easily)

Difficulties in mathematics are often major obstacles in the academic paths of students with learning disabilities, as they frequently continue to cause problems throughout high school. Mastery of fundamental quantitative concepts is vital to learning more abstract and complex mathematics, a requirement for students who seek to complete high school and attend colleges or universities (Cirino, Morris, & Morris, 2002, cited in Hardman et al., 2005). Further research on difficulties with mathematics and on effective instruction for students who encounter such problems grows more important as such young people seek to achieve more challenging educational goals (Hardman et al., p. 178).

Given these difficulties, it is not surprising that 50 percent of students with learning disabilities have individualized education program (IEP) goals in math. As with reading and writing, explicit, systematic instruction that provides guided, meaningful practice with feedback usually improves the math performance of students with learning disabilities (Fuchs, 2001, cited in Heward, 2005).

Dysgraphia (Writing Disorders)

Dysgraphia is a neurological disorder characterized by writing disabilities (Pierangelo & Giuliani, 2006). Specifically, the disorder causes a person's writing to be distorted or incorrect. In children, the disorder generally emerges when they are introduced to writing. They make inappropriately sized and spaced letters or write wrong or misspelled words, despite thorough instruction (National Institute of Neurological Disorders and Strokes, 2006).

Diagnostic symptoms of dysgraphia include the following (International Dyslexia Association, 2000):

- Generally illegible writing (despite appropriate time and attention given the task)
- Inconsistencies: mixtures of print and cursive or upper- and lowercase letters or irregular sizes, shapes, or slants of letters
- Unfinished words or letters; omitted words
- Inconsistent position on page with respect to lines and margins
- Inconsistent spaces between words and letters
- Cramped or unusual grip, especially the following:
  o Holding the writing instrument very close to the paper
  o Holding thumb over two fingers and writing from the wrist
  o Strange wrist, body, or paper position
- Talking to self while writing or carefully watching the hand that is writing
- Slow or labored copying or writing, even if the result is neat and legible
- Content that does not reflect the student's other language skills
- Combination of fine-motor difficulty, inability to revisualize letters, and inability to remember the motor patterns involved with writing

Students' handwriting problems can arise from their lack of fine-motor coordination, failure to attend to task, inability to perceive and/or remember visual images accurately, or inadequate handwriting instruction in the classroom (Friend & Bursuck, 2002, cited in Turnbull et al., 2004).

Many students struggle to produce neat, expressive written work, whether or not they have accompanying physical or cognitive difficulties. They may learn much less from an assignment because they must focus on writing mechanics instead of content. After spending more time on an assignment than their peers, these students understand the material less. Not surprisingly, belief in their ability to learn suffers. When the writing task is the primary barrier to learning or demonstrating knowledge, then accommodations, modifications, and remediation for these problems may be in order (Jones, 1999; Library of Congress, 2000).

Dyslexia (Reading Disorders)

Dyslexia is the learning disability associated with reading (Pierangelo & Giuliani, 2006). According to the National Center for Learning Disabilities (2008),

> dyslexia is a life-long language processing disorder that hinders the development of oral and written language skills. Children and adults with dyslexia can be highly intelligent, however they have a neurological disorder that causes the brain to process and interpret information differently.

According to the International Dyslexia Association (2007), diagnostic symptoms of dyslexia vary based on the age and grade level of the child. Listed below are the possible diagnostic symptoms of dyslexia for preschoolers to adults (Hallahan & Kauffman, 2006; International Dyslexia Association; Lerner, 2002; Pierangelo & Giuliani, 2006; Spafford & Grosser, 2005):

- Has trouble learning the alphabet, rhyming words, or connecting letters to their sounds
- Makes many mistakes when reading aloud and repeats and pauses often
- Does not understand what is read
- Has exceptional difficulty with spelling
- Learns language late and has a limited vocabulary
- Has trouble remembering the sounds that letters make or hearing slight differences between words
- Has trouble understanding jokes, comic strips, and sarcasm
- Has trouble following directions
- Mispronounces words or uses a wrong word that sounds similar

- Has trouble organizing what he or she wants to say or cannot think of the word needed for writing or conversation
- Does not follow the social rules of conversation, such as taking turns, and may stand too close to the listener
- Confuses math symbols and misreads numbers
- Cannot retell a story in order (what happened first, second, third)
- Does not know where to begin a task or how to go on from there

Dyslexia is a brain-based type of learning disability that specifically impairs a person's ability to read (Pierangelo & Giuliani, 2006). These individuals typically read at levels significantly lower than expected, despite having normal intelligence. Although the disorder varies from person to person, common characteristics among people with dyslexia are difficulties with phonological processing (the manipulation of sounds) and/or rapid visual-verbal responding (National Institute of Neurological Disorders and Strokes, 2007).

Dysorthographia (Spelling Disorders)

Dysorthographia is the learning disability associated with spelling (Akron's Children's Hospital, 2003; Pierangelo & Giuliani, 2006). Spelling is the ability to use letters to construct words in accordance with accepted usage. Spelling ability is viewed by some teachers and school administrators as equally important as other academic skills. Being a poor speller does not necessarily mean that a child has a learning disability. However, when poor spelling occurs with poor reading and/or arithmetic, then there may be reason for concern (Pierangelo & Giuliani).

Diagnostic symptoms of dysorthographia include the following (Hallahan & Kauffman, 2006; Turnbull et al., 2004):

- Addition of unneeded letters
- Omission of needed letters
- Reversals of vowels
- Reversals of syllables
- Phonemic spelling of nonphonemic words
- Difficulty in understanding the correspondence between sounds and letters

Spelling problems, like reading problems, originate with language learning weaknesses. Spelling disability does not reflect a general "visual memory" problem but a more specific problem with awareness of and memory for language structure, including the letters in words (Pierangelo & Giuliani, 2006).

Nonverbal Learning Disabilities (NLD)

Nonverbal learning disorder, also known as NLD, is a neurophysiological disorder originating in the right hemisphere of the brain. Reception of nonverbal or performance-based information governed by this hemisphere is impaired in varying degrees, resulting in problems that include the visual-spatial, intuitive, organizational, evaluative, and holistic processing functions (Nonverbal Learning Disorders Association, 2005).

Diagnostic symptoms for nonverbal learning disabilities include the following:

- Deficits in the areas of nonverbal problem solving, concept formation, or hypothesis testing
- Difficulty dealing with negative feedback in novel or complex situations
- Difficulties in dealing with cause-effect relationships
- Difficulties in the appreciation of incongruities
- Well-developed rote verbal capacities and rote verbal memory skills
- Overreliance on prosaic rote, and consequently inappropriate, behaviors in unfamiliar situations
- Relative deficiencies in mechanical arithmetic as compared to proficiencies in reading (word recognition) and spelling
- Rote and repetitive verbosity
- Content disorders of language
- Poor psycholinguistic pragmatics (cocktail party speech)
- Poor speech prosody
- Reliance on language for social relating, information gathering, and relief from anxiety
- Misspelling almost exclusively of the phonetically accurate variety
- Significant deficits in social perception, social judgment, and social interaction skills
- Marked tendency for social withdrawal and isolation as age increases
- High risk for social-emotional disturbance if no appropriate intervention is undertaken (Nonverbal Learning Disorders Association, 2005)

The interpersonal and social aspects of NLD have great significance for a student's life. The individual who does not attend to or accurately interpret the nonverbal communication of others cannot receive a clear message. Our concept of self is shaped in large measure by the reflection of how others view us. The person who has NLD, then, may not receive feedback from others and may suffer from a less clear concept of self.

The diminished ability to engage with others greatly limits the possibility of defining oneself based on such feedback.

Because of their verbal strengths, many individuals with NLD succeed in formal educational situations. However, if their social competence has not developed commensurately, they may not find and keep employment at the level for which their education has prepared them. On a positive note, individuals with NLD make considerable progress in areas of weakness when instruction is appropriate; accurate diagnosis and appropriate instruction can have great benefit for their lives (Foss, 2001).

Organizational Learning Disorders

An organizational learning disorder is a type of learning disability specifically associated with difficulties in organization. Children with this disorder may require constant support in organizing, arranging, setting priorities, and establishing time management when it comes to school tasks.

The diagnostic symptoms of an organizational disorder include difficulties with the following tasks:

- Temporal-sequential disorganization
- Allocating and estimating time
- Following schedules
- Meeting deadlines
- Solving problems in stages
- Material-spatial organization
- Keeping track of possessions
- Maintaining notebooks
- Arranging desks
- Finding objects like pencils and books
- Settling down and functioning effectively when expectations or settings change
- Remembering what one is required to do (Levine, 1995)

Developing good organizational skills is a key ingredient for success in school and in life. Although some people by nature are more organized than others, anyone can put routines and systems in place to help a child become more organized (LDOnline, n.d.). Chronic disorganization is a handicap that often goes unnamed throughout a child's entire school career. Yet it accompanies other learning disabilities in slightly more than half of the cases surveyed. For most children with chronic disorganization, the causes are neurological. Further, children with chronic disorganization may require daily coaching. Less frequent help is often not effective (Shwarzbeck, 2000).

Social Cue Disorder

Individuals with social cue disorder have difficulties in behaving in an automatic way. This is a problem with the self-governing part of the brain that stops one from doing such things as laughing at the wrong time, talking aloud to oneself, or coughing without covering the mouth. Students with this disorder might abruptly interrupt a conversation or talk aloud to themselves in public. Social interactions require a child to interpret, or "read," what other people communicate. Picking up on spoken and unspoken cues is a complex process. Having read another person's social cues, a child must next process the information, extract meaning, and decide how to respond effectively.

Diagnostic symptoms of children with social cue difficulties include the following (Giler, 2000):

- Inability to read facial expressions or body language (kinesis)
- Misinterpreting the use and meaning of pitch (vocalics)
- Misunderstanding the use of personal space (proxemics)

According to the Learning Disabilities Association (2005), individuals who have learning disabilities may be less observant in their social environment, may misinterpret the social behavior of others at times, and may not learn as easily from experiences or social cues as their friends. Some children may exhibit an immaturity and social ineptness due to their learning disability. While seeking acceptance, their eagerness may cause them to try too hard in inappropriate ways. Consequently, this problem may manifest itself in the following symptoms:

- Inability to interpret environment and social cues
- Poor judgment; little thought about logical consequences
- Poor impulse control
- Need for immediate gratification
- Inability to set realistic priorities and goals
- Inappropriate conclusions due to deficient reasoning ability
- Illogical reasons for actions
- Inability to develop meaningful relationships with others
- Immature and "bossy" behavior
- Low frustration tolerance, resulting in disruptive behavior

It should be noted that this disorder may best be determined by a professional trained in social behavior after careful observation in several different settings over a period of time, review of the child's social and developmental history, teacher interviews, and interviews with the parent(s). Perhaps the school psychologist or a clinical psychologist may be the best individual to determine the presence of this condition.

Visual Processing Disorders

A visual processing, or perceptual, disorder refers to a hindered ability to make sense of information taken in through the eyes. This is different from problems involving sight or sharpness of vision. Difficulties with visual processing affect how visual information is interpreted or processed by the brain (National Center for Learning Disabilities, 1999).

Diagnostic symptoms of individuals with visual processing disorders vary with age and grade level. Common symptoms in early childhood include the following (National Center on Learning Disabilities, 1999):

- Misunderstanding or confusing written symbols (e.g., +, ×, /, &)
- Being easily distracted, especially by competing visual information
- Writing within margins or on lines or misaligning numbers in math problems
- Misjudging distances (e.g., bumping into things or placing objects too close to an edge)
- Exhibiting a lack of fluidity of movement (e.g., not getting out of the way of a moving ball or knocking things over)
- Not differentiating colors or similarly shaped letters and numbers (e.g., *b* and *d*, *p* and *q*, *6* and *9*, or *2* and *5*)

Common symptoms of visual processing disorders in school-age children include difficulties with the following:

- Organizing and solving math problems
- Finding and retaining important information in reading assignments or tests
- Writing coherent, well-organized essays
- Copying from board or books
- Sewing or other types of fine-motor activities
- Writing neatly and quickly
- Reading with speed and precision

Symptoms of visual processing disorders in adults include difficulties with these activities:

- Accurately identifying information from pictures, charts, graphs, maps, etc.
- Organizing information from different sources into a single cohesive document
- Finding specific information on a printed page (e.g., getting a number out of the phone book)
- Remembering directions to a location

Interventions need to be aimed at the specific needs of the child. No two children share the same set of strengths or areas of weakness. An effective intervention utilizes a child's strengths to build on the specific areas in need of development. As such, interventions need to be viewed as a dynamic and ever-changing process. Although this may sound overwhelming initially, it is important to remember that the process of finding successful interventions becomes easier with time and as the child's learning approach, style, and abilities become more easily seen (National Center for Learning Disabilities, 1999).

4

Eligibility Criteria for Learning Disabilities

Step I: Becoming Familiar With the Characteristics of Students With Specific Learning Disabilities

There is no one sign that shows a person has a learning disability. Generally, experts look for a noticeable difference between how well a student does in school and how well that student *could* do, given the child's intelligence or ability. Also, certain clues may indicate that a student has a learning disability. Most relate to elementary school tasks, because learning disabilities tend to be identified in elementary school. A student probably won't show all of these signs or even most of them. However, if a student shows a number of these problems, then parent/guardians and the teacher should consider the possibility that the student has a learning disability.

When students have a learning disability, they may have the following challenges:

- Having trouble learning the alphabet, rhyming words, or connecting letters to their sounds
- Making many mistakes when reading aloud and repeating and pausing often

- Not understanding what is read
- Having exceptional trouble with spelling
- Having very messy handwriting or holding a pencil awkwardly
- Struggling to express ideas in writing
- Learning language late and having a limited vocabulary
- Having trouble remembering the sounds that letters make or hearing slight differences between words
- Having trouble understanding jokes, comic strips, and sarcasm
- Having trouble following directions
- Mispronouncing words or using a wrong word that sounds similar
- Having trouble organizing what they want to say or not being able to think of the word needed for writing or conversation
- Not following the social rules of conversation, such as taking turns, and standing too close to the listener
- Confusing math symbols and misreading numbers
- Not being able to retell a story in order (what happened first, second, third)
- Not knowing where to begin a task or how to go on from there

If a student has unexpected problems learning to read, write, listen, speak, or do math, then teachers and parent/guardians may want to investigate more. The same is true if the student is struggling to do any one of these skills. The student may need to be evaluated to see if he or she has a learning disability.

For more information on the characteristics of students with learning disabilities, see Chapter 2.

Step II: Determining the Procedures and Assessment Measures to Be Used

If a student is suspected of having a specific learning disability, the following evaluations should be considered:

- An observation by a team member, other than the student's general education teacher, of the student's academic performance in a general classroom setting or, in the case of a student less than school-age or out of school, an observation by a team member conducted in an age-appropriate environment
- A developmental history, if needed
- An assessment of intellectual ability

- Other assessments of the characteristics of learning disabilities if the student exhibits impairments in any one or more of the following areas: cognition, fine-motor skills, perceptual motor skills, communication, social or emotional skills, and perception or memory. These assessments should be completed by specialists knowledgeable in the specific characteristics being assessed.
- A review of cumulative records, previous individualized education programs, or individualized family service plans and teacher-collected work samples
- If deemed necessary, a medical statement or health assessment statement indicating whether any physical factors may be affecting the student's educational performance

Assessments to determine the impact of the suspected disability should measure the following:

- The student's educational performance when the student is at the age of eligibility for kindergarten through age 21
- The student's developmental progress when the student is age three through the age of eligibility for kindergarten
- Additional evaluations or assessments as necessary to identify the student's educational needs

At least one observation is required as part of the evaluation for determining a specific learning disability. Minimal observation requirements include the following:

- At least one team member other than the student's general education teacher must observe the student's academic performance in the general classroom setting. In the case of a student less than school age or out of school, a team member shall observe the student in an environment appropriate for a student of that age.
- The observer must note the relevant behavior noted and the relationship of that behavior to the student's academic functioning.

The evaluation must also include documentation that the student's learning problems are not primarily due to the following factors:

- Lack of appropriate instruction in reading and math
- Limited English proficiency
- Visual, hearing, or motor impairment
- Mental retardation
- Emotional disturbance

- Environmental, cultural, or economic disadvantage
- Motivational factors
- Situational traumas

Step III: Determination of Eligibility for a Diagnosis of a Specific Learning Disability

In general, states use two different methods to determine whether a student meets the eligibility criteria as a student with a specific learning disability under IDEA. We present a synopsis of these two options for an individualized education program (IEP) committee to consider.

Option 1

To identify and be determined as eligible for special education services as a student with a specific learning disability, the IEP committee shall document that the following standards have been met based on the results of the assessment:

- The student demonstrates a continued lack of progress when provided with appropriate instruction in the suspected area of disability.
- Documented evidence indicates that effective general education interventions and strategies have been attempted over a reasonable period of time.
- The determining factor for identification of a learning disability is not due to a lack of appropriate instruction in reading and math.
- Evidence exists that the student does not achieve commensurate with the child's age and ability in one or more of the following areas: listening comprehension, oral expression, basic reading skills, reading comprehension, written expression, mathematics calculation, and/or mathematics reasoning.
- A severe discrepancy exists between the student's educational performance and the student's achievement predicted on the basis of the best measure of cognitive ability. (This is an *optional consideration* under IDEA 2004.) Cognitive ability/achievement discrepancies should be used cautiously, because a learning disability can exist when a numerical discrepancy does not. Such comparisons may assist in the diagnostic process. Careful diagnosticians examine all information and recognize developmental factors, including age and academic experience, in making a determination as to the value of such discrepancies.

- There is evidence of a cognitive processing disorder that adversely affects the student's academic achievement. A *cognitive processing disorder* is defined as a deficit in the manner in which a student receives, stores, transforms, retrieves, and expresses information. Documented evidence exists that demonstrates or expresses the manifestation of the processing disorder in the identified achievement deficit.
- Evidence exists that the student's learning problems are not due primarily to visual, hearing, or motor impairments; mental retardation; emotional disturbance; environmental, cultural, or economic disadvantage; limited English proficiency; motivational factors; or situational traumas.
- There is evidence that characteristics as defined above are present and that the severity of the student's specific learning disability adversely affects the student's progress in the general education curriculum, demonstrating the need for special education and related services, and that students who perform in classroom academics in a manner commensurate with expected academic standards at the student's grade level cannot be considered as having a specific learning disability, even though they may show deficits on achievement tests in one or more of the seven academic areas.

Option 2

The team shall determine that a pupil has a specific learning disability and is in need of special education and related services when the pupil meets the criteria described in items A through C below. Information about each item must be sought from the parent/guardian and included as part of the assessment data. The assessment data must confirm that the disabling effects of the pupil's disability occur in a variety of settings.

A. The pupil must demonstrate severe underachievement in response to usual classroom instruction. The performance measures used to verify this finding must be both representative of the pupil's curriculum and useful for developing instructional goals and objectives. The following assessment procedures are required at a minimum to verify this finding:

1. Evidence of low achievement from sources such as cumulative record reviews, classwork samples, anecdotal teacher records, formal and informal tests, and curriculum based assessment results

2. Observation by at least one team member other than the pupil's general education teacher of the pupil's academic performance in the general classroom setting. In the case of a student served through an early childhood special education program or who is out of school, a team member shall observe the student in an environment appropriate for a student of that age.

B. The pupil must demonstrate a severe discrepancy between general intellectual ability and achievement in one or more of the following areas: oral expression, listening comprehension, written expression, basic reading skills, reading comprehension, mathematical calculation, or mathematical reasoning. The demonstration of a severe discrepancy shall not be based solely on the use of standardized tests. The team shall consider these standardized test results as only one component of the eligibility criteria.

1. The instruments used to assess the pupil's general intellectual ability and achievement must be individually administered and interpreted by an appropriately licensed person using standardized procedures.

2. For initial placement, the severe discrepancy must be at least 1.75 standard deviations below the mean of the distribution of difference scores for the general population of individuals at the pupil's chronological age level.

C. The team must agree that it has sufficient assessment data that verify the following conclusions:

1. The pupil has an information-processing condition that is manifested by such behaviors as inadequate or absent organizational skills (such as in following written and oral directions, spatial arrangements, correct use of developmental order in relating events, transfer of information onto paper), memory (visual and auditory), expression (verbal and nonverbal), and motor control for written tasks (such as pencil-and-paper assignments, drawing, and copying).

2. The disabling effects of the pupil's information processing condition occur in a variety of settings.

3. The pupil's underachievement is not primarily the result of vision, hearing, or motor impairment; mental impairment; emotional or behavioral disorders; environmental, cultural, economic influences; or a history of an inconsistent education program.

Key Points to Remember When Determining Eligibility for LD

Ongoing assessment throughout the school years is critical to develop the educational potential of all students, especially those with learning disabilities. School personnel, parent/guardians, and students should proceed with as much information as possible, giving consideration to individual skills and academic needs.

The recent explosion in brain research is beginning to impact teaching practices and address the differences in brain anatomy and chemistry in students with LD. Some current findings include insights on causation, hemispheric functioning, writing dysfunctions, dyslexia, and laterality. Overall, there is now scientific support for some LD characteristics that were previously identified mainly through observation and testing. Other information found in these studies suggests that LD teachers need to change some teaching practices based on brain research. As time goes on, there will be advances in identifying even more patterns of thinking in students with LD.

Given the enormous variability in the population of students with learning disabilities, the proliferation of tests on the market, and the problems cited above that are inherent in applying the definition, it has been extremely difficult to identify specific assessment instruments that consistently and appropriately identify these students. The problem of distinguishing students with LD from students without LD has become even more compounded by recent research that suggests that poor readers without disabilities and students who have been identified with mild learning disabilities may not differ significantly in the areas of information processing, genetics, or neurophysiological characteristics.

5

Response to Intervention (RTI)

The Response to Intervention (RTI) process is a multitiered approach to providing services and interventions to struggling learners at increasing levels of intensity. RTI can be used for making decisions about general, compensatory, and special education, creating a well-integrated and seamless system of instruction and intervention guided by child outcome data. RTI calls for early identification of learning and behavioral needs, close collaboration among teachers and special education personnel and parents, and a systemic commitment to locating and employing the necessary resources to ensure that students make progress in the general education curriculum. RTI is an initiative that takes place in the general education environment.

The National Research Center on Learning Disabilities (NRCLD, 2006) defines RTI as "an assessment and intervention process for systematically monitoring student progress and making decisions about the need for instructional modifications or increasingly intensified services using progress-monitoring data."

RTI is an integrated approach to service delivery that encompasses general, remedial, and special education through a multitiered service delivery model. It utilizes a problem-solving framework to identify and address academic and behavioral difficulties for all students through scientific, research-based instruction. Essentially, RTI is the practice of (a) providing high-quality instruction/intervention matched to all student needs and (b) using learning rate over time and level of performance to (c) make important educational decisions to guide instruction (National Association of State Directors of Special Education [NASDSE], 2005). RTI practices are proactive, incorporating both prevention and intervention, and are effective at all levels from early childhood through high school.

Purpose of RTI

RTI is intended to reduce the incidence of "instructional casualties" by ensuring that students are provided high-quality instruction with fidelity. By using RTI, districts can provide interventions to students as soon as a need arises. This is very different, for example, from the methods associated with the aptitude achievement discrepancy models traditionally utilized for LD identification, which have been criticized as a "wait to fail" approach.

IDEA 2004 allows the use of a student's "response to scientific, research-based intervention" (34 C.F.R. § 300.307[a][3]) as part of an evaluation. RTI functions as an alternative for learning disability evaluations within the general evaluation requirements of IDEA 2004. The statute continues to include requirements that apply to all disability categories, such as the use of validated, nonbiased methods and evaluation in all suspected areas of difficulty. IDEA 2004 added a new concept in eligibility that prohibits children from being found eligible for special education if they have not received instruction in reading that includes the five essential components of reading instruction identified by the Reading First Program. These requirements are those recognized by the National Reading Panel: phonemic awareness, phonics, reading fluency (including oral reading skills), vocabulary development, and reading comprehension strategies. RTI is included under this general umbrella. By using RTI, it is possible to identify students early, reduce referral bias, and test various theories for why a child is failing. It was included in the law specifically to offer an alternative to discrepancy models.

A key element of an RTI approach is the provision of early intervention when students first experience academic difficulties with the goal of improving the achievement of all students, including those who may have LD. In addition to the preventive and remedial services this approach may provide to at-risk students, it shows promise for contributing data useful for identifying LD. Thus, a student exhibiting (1) significantly low achievement and (2) insufficient RTI may be regarded as being at risk for LD and, in turn, as possibly in need of special education and related services. The assumption behind this paradigm, which has been referred to as a dual discrepancy (Fuchs, Fuchs, & Speece, 2002), is that when provided with quality instruction and remedial services, a student without disabilities will make satisfactory progress.

The concept of RTI has always been the focus of the teaching/ learning process and a basic component of accountability in general education: In other words, does instruction (i.e., strategies, methods, interventions, or curriculum) lead to increased learning and appropriate progress? In the past few years, RTI has taken on a more specific connotation, especially in IDEA 2004, as an approach to remedial intervention that also generates data to inform instruction and identify students who may require special education and related services. Today, many educators, researchers, and other professionals are exploring the usefulness of an RTI approach as an alternative that can provide (1) data for more effective and earlier identification of students with LD and (2) a systematic way to ensure that students experiencing educational difficulties receive more timely and effective support (Gresham, 2002; Learning Disabilities Roundtable, 2002, 2005; National Research Council, 2002; President's Commission on Excellence in Special Education, 2002).

Importance of RTI

According to current early reading research, all except a very few children can become competent readers by the end of the third grade. RTI is a process that provides immediate intervention to struggling students at the first indication of failure to learn. Through systematic screening of all students in the early grades, classroom teachers identify those who are not mastering critical reading skills and provide differentiated intervention to small groups of students. Continuous progress monitoring of students' responses to those interventions allows teachers to identify students in need of additional intervention and to adjust instruction accordingly.

Response to Intervention is about building better readers in the early grades and consists of multitiered reading instruction in the general education classroom. In an RTI model, *all* students receive high-quality reading instruction, and struggling readers receive additional and increasingly more intense intervention. Early intervention and prevention of reading difficulties are fundamental to the process. However, if a student's learning history and classroom performance warrant, a multidisciplinary team may determine the student has a disability and needs special education services to ensure continued and appropriate academic progress.

Three major developments concerning the education of students with learning problems have coalesced to establish RTI as a promising approach. First, long-standing concerns about the inadequacies of the ability-achievement discrepancy criterion—which was a component of identifying LD in the Individuals with Disabilities Education Act of 1997—have accentuated the need to develop alternative mechanisms for the identification of LD. At the August 2001 LD Summit, sponsored by the Office of Special Education Programs, RTI was the alternative proposed by several researchers (e.g., Gresham, 2002; Marston, 2001).

Second, special education has been used to serve struggling learners who do not have LD or other disabilities. An RTI approach has been suggested as a way to reduce referrals to special education by providing well-designed instruction and intensified interventions in general education, thereby distinguishing between students who perform poorly in school due to factors such as inadequate prior instruction from students with LD who need more intensive and specialized instruction.

A third major reason for the increased interest in an RTI approach has been the abundance of recent research on reading difficulties, in particular the national network of research studies coordinated by the National Institute of Child Health and Human Development (NICHD). A number of NICHD research studies have demonstrated that well-designed instructional programs or approaches result in significant improvements for the majority of students with early reading.

Is RTI a "New Approach"?

RTI is not a new approach. It is recognizable under other names, such as "dynamic assessment," "diagnostic teaching," and "precision teaching." Those terms, however, have been applied to approaches used to maximize student progress through sensitive measurement of the effects of instruction. RTI applies similar methods to draw conclusions and make LD classification decisions about students. The underlying assumption is that using RTI will identify children whose intrinsic difficulties make them the most difficult to teach. Engaging a student in a dynamic process like RTI provides an opportunity to assess various hypotheses about the causes of a child's difficulties, such as motivation or constitutional factors like attention.

Core Principles of RTI

RTI comprises seven core principles that represent recommended RTI practices (Mellard, 2004). These principles represent systems that must be in place to ensure effective implementation of RTI systems and establish a framework to guide and define the practice.

1. Use all available resources to teach all students.

RTI practices are built on the belief that all students can learn. One of the biggest changes associated with RTI is that it requires educators to shift their thinking—from the student to the intervention. This means that the initial evaluation no longer focuses on "what is wrong with the student." Instead, the focus is on an examination of the curricular, instructional, and environmental variables that change inadequate learning progress. Once the correct set of intervention variables has been identified, schools must then provide the means and systems for delivering resources so that effective teaching and learning can occur. In doing so, schools must provide resources in a manner that is directly proportional to students' needs. This requires districts and schools to reconsider current resource allocation systems so that financial and other support structures for RTI practices can be established and sustained.

2. Use scientific, research-based interventions/instruction.

The critical element of RTI systems is the delivery of scientific, research-based interventions with fidelity in general, remedial, and special education. This means that the curriculum and instructional approaches must have a high probability of success for the majority of students. By using research-based practices, schools efficiently use time and resources and protect students from ineffective instructional and evaluative practices. Since instructional practices vary in efficacy, ensuring that the practices and curriculum have demonstrated validity is an important consideration in the selection of interventions. With the absence of definitive research, schools should implement promising practices, monitor their effectiveness, and modify implementation based on their results.

3. Monitor classroom performance.

General education teachers play a vital role in designing and providing high-quality instruction. Furthermore, they are in the best position to assess students' performance and progress against grade-level standards in the general education curriculum. This principle emphasizes the importance of general education teachers in monitoring student progress rather than waiting to determine how students are learning in relation to their same-aged peers until results of statewide or district-wide assessments are available.

4. Conduct universal screening/benchmarking.

School staff conduct universal screening in all core academic areas and behavior. Screening data on all students can provide an indication of an individual student's performance and progress compared to the peer group's performance and progress. These data form the basis for an initial examination of individual and group patterns on specific academic skills (e.g., identifying letters of the alphabet or reading a list of high-frequency words) as well as behavior skills (e.g., attendance, cooperation, tardiness, truancy, suspensions, and/or disciplinary actions). Universal screening is the least-intensive level of assessment completed within a RTI system and helps educators and parents identify students early who might be at risk. Since screening data may not be as reliable as other assessments, however, it is important to use multiple sources of evidence in inferring whether a student is at risk.

5. Use a multitier model of service delivery.

An RTI approach incorporates a multitiered model of service delivery in which each tier represents an increasingly intense level of services associated with increasing levels of learner needs. The system described in this book reflects a three-tiered design. All multitiered systems, regardless of the number of levels chosen, should yield the same practical effects and outcomes.

In a RTI system, all students receive instruction in the core curriculum supported by strategic and intensive interventions when needed. Therefore, all students, including those with disabilities, are found in Tiers I, II, and III. Important features, such as universal screening, progress monitoring, fidelity of implementation, and problem solving occur within each tier. The basic tiered model reflects what we know about students in school: Their instructional needs will vary. Thus, the nature of the academic or behavioral intervention changes at each tier, becoming more rigorous as the student moves through the tiers.

Tier I represents the largest group of students, approximately 80–90 percent, who are performing adequately within the core curriculum. Tier II comprises a smaller group of students, typically 5–10 percent of the student population. These students need strategic interventions to raise their achievement to proficiency or above based on a lack of response to interventions at Tier I. Tier III contains the fewest number of students, usually 1–5 percent. These students need intensive interventions for their learning to be appropriately supported (Pierangelo & Giuliani, 2007).

6. Make data-based decisions.

Decisions within an RTI system are made by teams using problem solving and/or standard treatment protocol techniques. The purpose of these teams is to find the best instructional approach for a student with an academic or behavioral problem. Problem solving and standard treatment protocol decision making provide a structure for using data to monitor student learning so that good decisions can be made at each tier with a high probability of success. When using the problem-solving method, teams answer four interrelated questions: (1) Is there a problem and what is it? (2) Why is it happening? (3) What are we going to do about it? (4) Did our interventions work? (NASDSE, 2005). Problem solving and standard treatment protocol techniques ensure that decisions about a student's needs are driven by the student's response to high-quality interventions.

7. Monitor progress frequently.

To determine if the intervention is working for a student, the decision-making team must establish and implement progress monitoring. Progress monitoring is the use of assessments that can be collected frequently and are sensitive to small changes in student behavior. Data collected through progress monitoring informs the decision-making team whether changes in instruction or goals are needed. Informed decisions about students' needs require frequent data collection to provide reliable measures of progress. Various curriculum-based measurements are useful tools for monitoring students' progress.

Events That Led to Changes in LD Identification in IDEA 2004

Through decades of educational practice, it has become generally accepted that a "severe discrepancy" is in fact a learning disability and/or a proxy for a learning disability and its underlying processing disorders. It is now widely acknowledged that no scientific basis exists for the use of a measured IQ achievement discrepancy as either a defining characteristic of or a marker for LD. Though numerous authorities (Fletcher et al., 1998; Lyon et al., 2001; Stanovich, 2005) have identified problems with discrepancy models, these models have persisted as the most widely used diagnostic concept. In the 1997 reauthorization process, the concern with discrepancy approaches reached a head, and the U.S. Office of Special Education Programs (OSEP) committed to a vigorous program of examining and summarizing evidence around LD identification. That effort resulted in the Learning Disabilities Summit, as well as subsequent roundtable meetings involving representatives of major professional organizations.

Rationale for Replacing the Discrepancy Model With RTI

Response to Intervention offers the promise of "building better readers" through the provision of differentiated instruction based on data from ongoing assessments for all students in the early grades. That is, all students receive scientific, research-based reading instruction, and most importantly, struggling readers receive additional instructional time and research-based reading interventions within the structure and context of the general education classroom. In essence, RTI replaces the practice of "waiting to fail" with deliberate early intervention and prevention.

Major Issues Related to the Use of the Concept of Achievement-Ability Discrepancy

Issue #1: Discrepancy models fail to differentiate between children who have LD and those who have academic achievement problems related to poor instruction, lack of experience, or other problems.

It is generally agreed that the model of achievement-ability discrepancy that has been employed was influenced by research conducted by Rutter and Yule (1975, cited in Reschly, Hosp, & Schmied, 2003). This research found two groups of low-achieving readers, one with discrepancies and one without. It was this finding that formed the basis for the idea that a discrepancy was meaningful for both classification and treatment purposes. Later analyses of this research and attempts to replicate it have failed to produce support for the "two-group" model for either purpose. In fact, it is now accepted that reading occurs in a normal distribution and that students with dyslexia or severe reading problems represent the lower end of that distribution (Fletcher et al., 2002).

Issue #2: Discrepancy models discriminate against certain groups of students: students outside of "mainstream" culture and students who are in the upper and lower ranges of IQ.

Due to psychometric problems, discrepancy approaches tend to underidentify children at the lower end of the IQ range and overidentify children at the upper end. This problem has been addressed by various formulas that correct for the regression to the mean that occurs when two correlated measures are used. However, using regression formulas does not address issues such as language and cultural bias in IQ tests, nor does it improve the classification function of a discrepancy model (Stuebing et al., 2002).

Issue #3: Discrepancy models do not effectively predict which students will benefit from or respond differentially to instruction.

The research around this issue has examined both progress and absolute outcomes for children with and without discrepancies and has not supported the notion the two groups will respond differentially to instruction (Stanovich, 2005). Poor readers with discrepancies and poor readers without discrepancies perform similarly on skills considered to be important to the development of reading skills (Gresham, 2002).

Issue #4: The use of discrepancy models requires children to fail for a substantial period of time—usually years—before they are far enough behind to exhibit a discrepancy.

For children to exhibit a discrepancy, two tests need to be administered—an IQ test, such as the Wechsler Intelligence Scale for Children, and an achievement test, such as one of the Woodcock Johnson Tests of Achievement. Because of limitations of achievement and IQ testing, discrepancies often do not "appear" until late-second, third, or even fourth grade. Educators and parents have experienced the frustration of knowing a child's skills are not adequate and not typical of the child's overall functioning yet being told to "wait a year" to re-refer the child. While concerned parties wait for a discrepancy to appear, other persistent problems associated with school failure develop, such as poor self-concept, compromised motivation, vocabulary deficits, and deficits associated with limited access to written content.

Why RTI Was Considered in the Process of LD Determination

RTI is being strongly considered as part of the specific learning disabilities (SLD) identification process because it has the potential to address areas of the SLD definition and construct that are not adequately assessed with current approaches. If the features of RTI are implemented correctly, it may accomplish the following:

- There is some assurance that students are being exposed to high-quality instruction in the general education classroom by stipulating that schools use evidence-based instructional practices and routinely monitor the progress of all students.
- Discrepancy models that examine whether a student is failing to respond to instruction through both measures of low overall achievement and inability to make adequate progress emphasize underachievement.
- RTI encourages access to early intervention because, with regular monitoring of progress, at-risk students are identified early and an infrastructure for the appropriate delivery of services already is established.
- RTI is designed to address many students with achievement problems, so the label of "learning disability" is applied only to those students who fail to respond to multiple levels of intervention efforts.
- RTI is meant to be applied via multiple measures of child performance rather than limiting determination to a single point in time.

The Role RTI Should Play in the Identification of Children With Specific Learning Disabilities

When considering adopting an RTI approach for identifying students with specific learning disabilities, school districts should keep in mind a number of provisions of IDEA 2004. Under IDEA 2004, schools districts may, but are no longer required to, consider whether a student has a severe discrepancy between achievement and intellectual ability. At the same time, IDEA 2004 gives school districts the flexibility to determine that a student has SLD using RTI data. Proponents point out that identifying SLD through RTI shifts the focus of the evaluation process from emphasizing the documentation of the student's disability to emphasizing the student's instructional needs. RTI emphasizes this shift of focus through documentation of a student's persistent failure to progress even after receiving intense and sound scientific, research-based interventions in the general education curriculum.

IDEA 2004 is silent about the exact criteria school districts may use in establishing SLD. It is expected that when final federal regulations are published, specific criteria will be established, and states will be provided clarifying guidance regarding these procedures. Until that time, districts implementing RTI are strongly encouraged to use established approaches for using RTI data to identify SLD. The following approach is recommended.

Identifying Special Learning Disabilities

After appropriate curriculum-based measurement (CBM) probes have been applied and after attempts have been made to implement at least two Tier III interventions with fidelity, students should be considered nonresponsive when their level of academic achievement has (a) been determined to be significantly lower than that of their peers and (b) the gap between the students' achievement and that of their peers increases (or does not significantly decrease). Absent other information to explain the lack of achievement, students who are nonresponsive at Tier III should be suspected of having a disability.

Once a referral for 504 or special education is initiated, the school district must determine whether or not an initial comprehensive evaluation is required to determine the presence of a disability. Unless mitigating information exists to explain why the student was nonresponsive at Tier III, it is anticipated that an initial evaluation will be completed. Before conducting an initial evaluation, the school district must obtain written consent from a parent or guardian. A comprehensive evaluation may or may not require additional testing. A comprehensive evaluation should include a formal observation of the student by a team member, unless a recent observation was completed by a team member prior to the evaluation. On the other hand, if the student's evaluation team is able to determine that the existing data developed through the RTI process is sufficient to complete the evaluation report in all suspected areas of disability, additional information does not need to be obtained. If the existing data does not establish the need for special education services, further assessment may be needed to rule out the possibility of a qualifying disability, including a disability in a category other than SLD.

Can RTI Be Used as the Sole Determinant for LD Classification?

While RTI addresses some significant shortcomings in current approaches to SLD identification and other concerns about early identification of students at risk for reading problems, RTI should be considered as merely *one* important element within the larger context of the SLD determination process. Implementing RTI allows schools to have more confidence that they are providing appropriate learning experiences to *all* students while identifying and targeting early those students who may be at risk for reading or math problems but who do not necessarily have a learning disability. Although IDEA 2004 provides flexibility to local education agencies (LEAs) in determining SLD identification procedures, the following recommendations by the National Joint Committee on Learning Disabilities (NJCLD) should help guide the development of these procedures (NJCLD, 2005):

> Decisions regarding eligibility for special education services must draw from information collected from a comprehensive individual evaluation using multiple methods including clinical judgment and other sources of relevant information. Students must be evaluated on an individual basis and assessed for intra-individual differences in the seven domains that comprise the definition of SLD in the law—listening, thinking, speaking, reading, writing, spelling, and mathematical calculation. Eligibility decisions must be made through an interdisciplinary team, must be student-centered and informed by appropriate data, and must be based on student needs and strengths.

As schools begin to execute a process of decision making that is more clinical than statistical in nature, ensuring through regulations that this team of qualified professionals represents all competencies necessary for accurate review of comprehensive assessment data will be critical.

One of the advantages of RTI is the timely identification of children who struggle with learning. While RTI is not intended as a stand-alone approach to determining specific learning disabilities, it can be a key component of a comprehensive approach to disability determination. In an RTI model, if a student does not respond to robust, high-quality instruction and intervention that is progress-monitored over time, the student may indeed be determined to have a learning disability. The benefit of RTI for these at-risk students is that it provides a wealth of meaningful instructional data that can be used in creating well-targeted individualized instructional programs and evidence-based instructional interventions. In addition, RTI sets in place a student progress-monitoring process that facilitates communication and promotes ongoing meaningful dialogue between home and school.

In the Big Picture, How Does RTI Fit Into the Process of Determining LD?

Although RTI addresses some significant shortcomings in current approaches to SLD identification and other concerns about early identification of students at risk for reading problems, RTI should be considered to be only one important element within the larger context of the SLD determination process. RTI, as one component of SLD determination, is insufficient as a sole criterion for accurately determining SLD. RTI provides the following information about a student:

- Indication of the student's skill level relative to peers or a criterion benchmark
- Success or lack of success of particular interventions
- Sense of the intensity of instructional supports that will be necessary for the student to achieve

Incorporating this information into SLD determination procedures can potentially make important contributions to identifying students with SLD. In addition to an RTI process that helps ensure appropriate learning experiences and early intervention, identification of SLD should include a student-centered, comprehensive evaluation that ensures accurate identification of students with learning disabilities.

Although IDEA 2004 provides flexibility to LEAs in determining SLD identification procedures, the following recommendations by the National Joint Committee on Learning Disabilities should help guide the development of these procedures (NJCLD, 2005):

- Decisions regarding eligibility for special education services must draw from information collected from a comprehensive individual evaluation using multiple methods, including clinical judgment and other sources of relevant information.
- Students must be evaluated on an individual basis and assessed for intra-individual differences in the seven domains that comprise the definition of SLD in the law: listening, thinking, speaking, reading, writing, spelling, and mathematical calculation.
- Eligibility decisions must be made through an interdisciplinary team, must be student centered and informed by appropriate data, and must be based on student needs and strengths.
- As schools begin to execute a process of decision making that is more clinical than statistical in nature, ensuring through regulations that this team of qualified professionals represents all competencies necessary for accurate review of comprehensive assessment data will be critical.

Processes for SLD identification have changed and will continue to do so. Within that context, remembering that RTI is but one resource for use in the SLD determination process is important. More broadly speaking, RTI procedures have the distinction that when implemented with fidelity, they can identify and intervene for students early in the educational process, thereby reducing academic failure.

Multitiered Service Delivery Model

Response to Intervention is a multitiered service delivery model. An RTI approach incorporates a multitiered model of educational service delivery in which each tier represents increasingly intense services that are associated with increasing levels of learner needs. The various tier interventions are designed to provide a set of curricular/instructional processes aimed at improving student response to instruction and student outcomes.

Much discussion continues surrounding the issues of how many tiers constitute an adequate intervention (O'Connor, Tilly, Vaughn, & Marston, 2003). Most frequently, RTI is viewed as a three-tiered model, similar to those used for other service delivery practices, such as positive behavioral support. Figure 5.1 depicts a three-tiered model as conceived in an RTI framework.

Like other models, RTI is meant to be applied on a schoolwide basis, with the majority of students receiving instruction in Tier I (the general classroom), students who are at risk for reading and other learning disabilities are identified (such as through school-wide screening) for more intense support in Tier II, and students who fail to respond to the interventions provided in Tier II may then be considered for specialized instruction in Tier III.

The application of RTI is typically understood within the context of a multitiered model or framework that delineates a continuum of programs and services for students with academic difficulties. Although no universally accepted model or approach currently exists, the many possible variations can be conceptualized as elaborations on or modifications of the following three-tiered model:

- *Tier I:* High-quality instructional and behavioral supports are provided for all students in general education.
  - ○ School personnel conduct universal screening of literacy skills, academics, and behavior.
  - ○ Teachers implement a variety of research-supported teaching strategies and approaches.
  - ○ Ongoing, curriculum-based assessment and continuous progress monitoring are used to guide high-quality instruction.

Figure 5.1   Continuum of Intervention Support for At-Risk Students

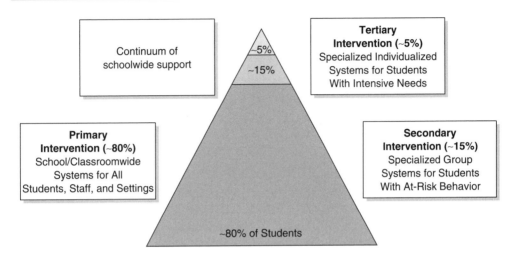

Source: U.S. Department of Education

- o Students receive differentiated instruction based on data from ongoing assessments.
- *Tier II:* Students whose performance and rate of progress lag behind those of peers in their classroom, school, or district receive more specialized prevention or remediation within general education.
  - o Curriculum-based measures are used to identify which students continue to need assistance and with what specific kinds of skills.
  - o Collaborative problem solving used to design and implement instructional support for students, which may consist of a standard protocol or more individualized strategies and interventions.
  - o Identified students receive more intensive scientific, research-based instruction targeted to their individual needs.
  - o Student progress is monitored frequently to determine intervention effectiveness and needed modifications.
  - o Systematic assessment is conducted to determine the fidelity or integrity with which instruction and interventions are implemented.
  - o Parents are informed and included in the planning and monitoring of their child's progress in Tier II specialized interventions.
  - o General education teachers receive support (e.g., training, consultation, direct services for students), as needed, from other

qualified educators in implementing interventions and monitoring student progress.

- *Tier III:* Comprehensive evaluation is conducted by a multidisciplinary team to determine eligibility for special education and related services.
  - o Parents are informed of their due process rights, and consent is obtained for the comprehensive evaluation needed to determine whether the student has a disability and is eligible for special education and related services.
  - o Evaluation uses multiple sources of assessment data, which may include data from standardized and norm-referenced measures; observations made by parents, students, and teachers; and data collected in Tiers I and II.
  - o Intensive, systematic, specialized instruction is provided, and additional RTI data are collected, as needed, in accordance with special education time lines and other mandates.
  - o Procedural safeguards concerning evaluations and eligibility determinations apply, as required by IDEA 2004 mandates.

Fuchs, Mock, Morgan, and Young (2003) used the term *standard protocol* to refer to an approach in which students with similar difficulties (e.g., problems with reading fluency) are given a research-based intervention that has been standardized and shown to be effective for students with similar difficulties and uses a standard protocol to ensure implementation integrity. The term *standard protocol* is used in the same sense in this book.

Variations on this basic framework may be illustrated by options often found within Tier II. For example, Tier II might consist of two hierarchical steps, or subtiers (e.g., a teacher first collaborates with a single colleague, then, if needed, problem-solves with a multidisciplinary team, creating in effect a four-tiered model). Alternatively, more than one type of intervention might be provided within Tier II (e.g., both a standard protocol and individualized planning, based on the student's apparent needs).

RTI is a critical component of a multitiered service delivery system. The goal of such a system is to ensure that quality instruction, good teaching practices, differentiated instruction, and remedial opportunities are available in general education and that special education is provided for students with disabilities who require more specialized services than can be provided in general education. The continuous monitoring of the adequacy of student response to instruction is particularly relevant to an RTI approach as a means of determining whether a student should move from one tier to the next by documenting that existing instruction and support is not sufficient. For example, in moving from Tier II to Tier III, insufficient responsiveness to high-quality, scientific, research-based intervention may be cause to suspect that a student has a disability and should be referred for a special education evaluation. In addition, however, the right of a parent, state education agency, or a local education agency to initiate a request for an evaluation at any time is maintained in IDEA 2004.

Focus of Tier I

Tier I is designed to meet the needs of a majority of the school population and has three critical elements:

1. A research-based core curriculum

2. Short-cycle assessments for all students at least three times a year to determine their instructional needs

3. Sustained professional development to equip teachers with tools necessary for teaching content effectively. In Tier I, the goal is to prevent failure and optimize learning by offering the most effective instruction possible to the greatest number of students. Instruction takes place in a regular education setting and is, for the most part, whole-class (and scientifically based) instruction that produces good results for most students. Based on data, classroom teachers monitor student progress and differentiate instruction for students who do not meet grade-level expectations.

Focus of Tier II

Tier II is for students who are falling behind same-age peers and need additional, targeted interventions to meet grade-level expectations. In Tier II, the goal is to accelerate learning for students who need more intensive support. In Tier II, interventions typically take place in a regular setting and may include instruction to small groups of students, targeted interventions, and frequent progress monitoring.

Focus of Tier III

Tier III is designed for students who still have considerable difficulty in mastering necessary academic and/or behavioral skills, even after Tier I and Tier II instruction and interventions. Tier III addresses students' needs through intensive individualized services. In Tier III, students receive intensive and highly focused, intentional, research-based instruction, possibly over a long period. Students also undergo a more formal diagnostic evaluation.

Parent Involvement: An Important Component of Successful RTI Programs

Involving parents at all phases is a key aspect of a successful RTI program. As members of the decision-making team, parents can provide a critical perspective on students, thus increasing the likelihood that RTI interventions will be effective. For this reason, schools must make a concerted effort to involve parents as early as possible, beginning with instruction in the core curriculum. This can be done through traditional methods, such as parent-teacher conferences and regularly scheduled meetings, or by other methods. Parents must be notified of student progress within the RTI system on a regular basis.

Districts and schools should provide parents with written information about the RTI program and be prepared to answer questions about RTI processes. The written information should explain how the system is different from a traditional education system and about the vital and collaborative role that parents play within a RTI system. The more parents are involved as players, the greater the opportunity for successful RTI outcomes.

Because RTI is a method of delivering the general education curriculum for all students, written consent is not required before administering universal screenings, curriculum-based measurements, and targeted assessments within a multitiered RTI system when these tools are used to determine instructional need. However, when a student fails to respond to interventions and the decision is made to evaluate a student for special education eligibility, written consent must be obtained in accordance with special education procedures. When developing screening measures, districts should also consider the parallel measures that may be used for evaluation.

Failure to communicate and reach out to parents will lead to confusion, especially among parents who believe their children have a learning disability. Schools may also want to provide other means for keeping parents engaged and informed:

- Involving them in state and local planning for RTI adoption
- Providing them written material informing them of their right to refer their children at any time for special education evaluation as stipulated in IDEA 2004

- Providing written material that outlines the criteria for determining eligibility under IDEA 2004 and the role of RTI data in making LD determinations

Taking measures to build strong, productive relationships with parents can only increase the likelihood that students will benefit greatly from a RTI model.

Fidelity

Fidelity refers to the degree to which RTI components are implemented as designed, intended, and planned. Fidelity is achieved through sufficient time allocation, adequate intervention intensity, qualified and trained staff, and sufficient materials and resources. Fidelity is vital in universal screening, instructional delivery, and progress monitoring.

The RTI Process for Teachers

An RTI outcome vital to the effectiveness of a school system is that *all* teachers, both general and special educators, feel an increased accountability for student learning, as well as strengthened confidence in their own skills and knowledge related to teaching reading. The goal of making sure that all students learn to read is a unifying force that includes all staff and all students. All teachers will see themselves as part of a system that delivers high-quality instruction that continually assesses student progress and provides extra help and extra time to meet the needs of students.

If we are to close the achievement gap in schools, roles of school personnel must change. Collaboration among teachers will increase to determine students' needs, designate resources, and maximize student learning. Genuine access to and participation in the general curriculum for students with disabilities may require a shift in the way we think about and ultimately provide special education and related services. Building better readers must become the collective responsibility of all teachers so that all students achieve.

Although RTI presents a promising way of addressing many issues associated with SLD identification, unanswered implementation questions remain. We must ask how many issues relevant to SLD determination are due to the specific assessment components as well as the limited fidelity with which those components are implemented (e.g., appropriate learning experiences, prereferral intervention, application of exclusion clause, and aptitude-achievement discrepancy). Further, we must consider how well states/districts/schools could implement an assessment process that incorporates significant changes in staff roles and responsibilities, most dramatically for general education staff, while lengthening the duration of disability determination assessment and possibly lengthening service time.

Another significant consideration is that current research literature provides scant scientific evidence for how RTI applies in curricular areas other than early reading and beyond primary or elementary school-age children. In conjunction with the standards that have been developed (National Committee on Science Education Standards and Assessment, National Research Council, 1996; National Council of Teachers of Mathematics [NCTM], 2000), science-based research needs to be conducted using the RTI construct in the areas of later reading (e.g., reading comprehension) as well as science and mathematics. Using an RTI framework across educational disciplines as well as grade levels is consonant with the No Child Left Behind Act of 2001 and promotes the value that schools have an obligation to ensure that all students participate in strong instructional programs that support multifaceted learning.

What Teachers Need in Terms of Professional Development and RTI

Teachers will need to acquire specialized knowledge to individualize instruction, build skills, and recommend modifications and accommodations needed for students with learning disabilities to be successful in the general curriculum.

Within the RTI framework, professional development will be needed to prepare these teachers to be able to achieve the following:

- Understand and apply pedagogy related to cognition, learning theory, language development, behavior management, and applied behavioral analysis
- Possess a substantial base of knowledge about criteria for identifying scientific, research-based methodology and instructional programs available for use with students with learning disabilities and individualization of instruction
- Be proficient in providing direct skill instruction in reading, writing, spelling, math, listening, and learning strategies
- Be able to adjust instruction and learning supports based on student progress, observation, and clinical judgment

- Conduct comprehensive evaluations that include standardized assessment measures, informal assessment, and behavioral observations, as well as translate the data into meaningful educational recommendations
- Explain test results to help parents and teachers understand each student's needs and the recommendations generated during the assessment process
- Possess strong communication skills to function as collaborative partners and members of problem-solving teams
- Be knowledgeable about the legal requirements of IDEA 2004, federal and state regulations, and the history of learning disabilities

6

Effective Teaching Strategies for Students With LD

Effective strategies for students with LD often emphasize all three of the following components:

1. Academic instruction

2. Behavioral interventions

3. Classroom accommodations

Academic Instruction

Prepare Students for Upcoming Lessons

Research suggests that students with LD learn best with a carefully structured academic lesson—one where the teacher explains what he or she wants students to learn in the current lesson and places these skills and knowledge in the context of previous lessons. A number of teaching-related practices have been found especially useful in facilitating this process:

- *Discuss and establish learning expectations:* State what students are expected to learn during the lesson. For example, explain to students that a language arts lesson will involve reading a story about Paul Bunyan and identifying new vocabulary words in the story.

- *Discuss and establish behavioral expectations:* Describe how students are expected to behave during the lesson. For example, tell students that they may talk quietly to their neighbors as they do their seatwork or they may raise their hands to get your attention.

- *Offer an advance organizer:* Prepare students for the day's lesson by quickly summarizing the order of the various activities planned. Explain, for example, that a review of the previous lesson will be followed by new information and that both group and independent work will be expected.

- *Take time out to review previous lessons:* Review information about previous lessons on this topic. For example, remind students that yesterday's lesson focused on learning how to regroup in subtraction. Review several problems before describing the current lesson.

- *Be very clear on materials needed:* Identify all materials that the students will need during the lesson rather than leaving them to figure out the required materials on their own. For example, specify that students need their journals and pencils for journal writing or their crayons, scissors, and colored paper for an art project.

- *Make instructions, choices, and scheduling as easy as possible:* The simpler the expectations communicated to an LD student, the more likely she will comprehend and complete them in a timely and productive manner.

Conducting Effective Lessons

The following set of strategies may assist teachers in conducting effective lessons:

- *Remember that reliability and predictability are essential.* Structure and consistency are very important for students with LD; many do not deal well with change. Minimal rules and minimal choices are best for these students. They need to understand clearly what is expected of them, as well as the consequences for not adhering to expectations.

- *Try to get the student to participate in the classroom.* Provide students with LD with private, discreet cues to stay on-task and advance warning that they will be called upon shortly. Avoid bringing attention to differences between LD students and their class-mates. At all times, avoid the use of sarcasm and criticism.

- *Utilize audiovisual materials.* Use a variety of audiovisual materials to present academic lessons. For example, use an overhead projector to demonstrate how to solve an addition problem requiring regrouping. The students can work on the problem at their desks while you manipulate counters on the projector screen.

- *Check student performance.* Question individual students to assess their mastery of the lesson. For example, you can ask students doing seatwork (i.e., lessons completed by students at their desks in the classroom) to demonstrate how they arrived at the answer to a problem, or you can ask individual students to state, in their own words, how the main character felt at the end of the story.

- *Try to ask probing questions.* Probe for the correct answer after allowing a student sufficient time to work out the answer to a question. Count at least 15 seconds before giving the answer or calling on another student. Ask follow-up questions that give students an opportunity to demonstrate what they know.

- *Assess students on an ongoing basis.* Identify students who need additional assistance. Watch for signs of lack of comprehension, such as daydreaming or visual or verbal indications of frustration. Provide these students with extra explanations or ask another student to serve as a peer tutor for the lesson.

- *Help students correct their own mistakes.* Describe how students can identify and correct their own mistakes. For example, remind students that they should check their calculations in math problems and reiterate how they can check their calculations, or remind students of particularly difficult spelling rules and how students can watch out for easy-to-make errors.

- *Help students focus.* Remind students to keep working and to focus on their assigned task. For example, you can provide follow-up directions or assign learning partners. These practices can be directed at individual students or at the entire class.

- *Provide follow-up directions.* Effective teachers of students with LD also guide them with follow-up directions:
  - *Oral directions:* After giving directions to the class as a whole, provide additional oral directions for a student with LD. For example, ask if the student understood the directions and repeat the directions together.
  - *Written directions:* Provide follow-up directions in writing. For example, write the page number for an assignment on the chalkboard and remind the student to look at the chalkboard if he or she forgets the assignment.

- *Reduce the noise level.* Monitor the noise level in the classroom and provide corrective feedback as needed. If the noise level exceeds that appropriate for the type of lesson, remind all students—or individual students—about the behavioral rules stated at the beginning of the lesson.
- *Simplify work into smaller units.* Break down assignments into smaller, less complex tasks. For example, allow students to complete five math problems before presenting them with the remaining five problems.
- *Emphasize key points.* Highlight key words in the instructions on worksheets to help the student with LD focus on the directions. Prepare the worksheet before the lesson begins or underline key words as you and the student read the directions together. When reading, show students how to identify and highlight a key sentence, or have them write it on a separate piece of paper, before asking for a summary of the entire book. In math, show students how to underline the important facts and operations (e.g., in "Mary has two apples, and John has three," underline *two, and,* and *three*).
- *Avoid "high-pressure" and/or timed tests.* Tests that are timed may not allow students with LD to demonstrate what they truly know due to their potential preoccupation with elapsed time. Allow students with LD more time to complete quizzes and tests to reduce test anxiety, and provide them with other opportunities, methods, or test formats to demonstrate their knowledge.
- *Provide group work.* Have students work together in small groups to maximize their own and each other's learning. Use strategies such as "think-pair-share," where teachers ask students to think about a topic, pair with a partner to discuss it, and share ideas with the group.
- *Learn about and use assistive technology.* All students, and those with LD in particular, can benefit from the use of technology (such as computers and projector screens), which makes instruction more visual and allows students to participate actively.

In conclusion, the most effective manner in which teachers can conduct lessons for students with LD is by periodically questioning students' understanding of the material, probing for correct answers before calling on other students, and identifying which students need additional assistance. Educators should always remember that moving from one lesson or class to another is often particularly difficult for students with LD. The key lies in preparing students for the transition. When they are prepared for transitions, students with LD are more likely to respond and to stay on-task.

Concluding Lessons

Effective teachers of students with LD conclude their lessons by providing advance warning that the lesson is about to end, checking the completed assignments of at least some of the students with LD, and instructing students how to begin preparing for the next activity.

- *Give advance notice.* Provide advance warning that a lesson is about to end. Announce 5 or 10 minutes before the end of the lesson (particularly for seatwork and group projects) how much time remains. You may also want to tell students at the beginning of the lesson how much time they will have to complete it.
- *Go over assignments.* Check completed assignments for at least some students. Review what they have learned during the lesson to get a sense of how ready the class was for the lesson and how to plan the next lesson.
- *Be sure to take some time to preview the next lesson.* Instruct students on how to begin preparing for the next lesson. For example, inform students that they need to put away their textbooks and come to the front of the room for a large-group spelling lesson.

Individualizing Instructional Practices

In addition to the general strategies listed above for introducing, conducting, and concluding their lessons, effective teachers of students with LD individualize their instructional practices in accordance with different academic subjects and the needs of their students within each area. This is because students with LD have different ways of learning and retaining information, not all of which involve traditional reading and listening. Effective teachers first identify areas in which each student requires extra assistance and then use special strategies to provide structured opportunities for the student to review and master an academic lesson that was previously presented to the entire class. Strategies that may help facilitate this goal include the following (grouped by subject area).

Language Arts and Reading Comprehension

To help students with LD who are poor readers improve their reading comprehension skills, try the following instructional practices:

- *·Provide silent reading time.* Establish a fixed time each day for silent reading. Examples of potentially effective approaches are D.E.A.R.

(Drop Everything and Read) and Sustained Silent Reading (Holt & O'Tuel, 1989; Manzo & Zehr, 1998).

- *Provide follow-along reading.* Ask the student to read a story silently while listening to other students or the teacher read the story aloud to the entire class.
- *Provide partner reading activities.* Pair the student with LD with another student who is a strong reader. The partners take turns reading orally and listening to each other.
- *Teach the student how to make a storyboard.* Ask the student to make storyboards that illustrate the sequence of main events in a story.
- *Schedule storytelling.* Schedule storytelling sessions where the student can retell a story that the student has read recently.
- *Schedule playacting.* Schedule playacting sessions where the student can role-play different characters in a favorite story.
- *Keep a word bank.* Keep a word bank or dictionary of new or "hard-to-read" sight-vocabulary words.
- *Play board games for reading comprehension.* Play board games that provide practice with target reading comprehension skills or sight-vocabulary words.
- *Schedule computer games for reading comprehension.* Schedule computer time for the student to have drill-and-practice with sight-vocabulary words.
- *Utilize recorded books.* These materials, available from many libraries, can stimulate interest in traditional reading and can be used to reinforce and complement reading lessons.
- *Have "backup" materials for home use.* Make available to students a second set of books and materials that they can keep at home and use there.
- *Provide summary materials.* Allow and encourage students to use published book summaries, synopses, and digests of major reading assignments to review (not replace) reading assignments.

Phonics

To help students with LD master rules of phonics, the following approaches are effective:

- *Teach the student mnemonics for phonics.* Teach the student mnemonics that provide reminders about hard-to-learn phonics rules (e.g., "When two vowels go walking, the first does the talking.") (Scruggs & Mastropieri, 2000).

- *Teach word families.* Teach the student to recognize and read word families that illustrate particular phonetic concepts (e.g., /ph/ sounds, *at-bat-cat*).
- *Provide and play board games for phonics.* Have students play board games, such as bingo, that allow them to practice phonetically irregular words.
- *Use computer games for phonics.* Use a computer to provide opportunities for students to drill and practice with phonics or grammar lessons.
- *Use picture-letter charts.* Use these for students who know sounds but do not know the letters that go with them.

Writing

In composing stories or other writing assignments, students with LD benefit from the following practices:

- *Provide standards for writing assignments.* Identify and teach the student classroom standards for acceptable written work, such as format and style.
- *Teach students to recognize parts of a story.* Teach the student how to describe the major parts of a story (e.g., plot, main characters, setting, conflict, and resolution). Use a storyboard with parts listed for this purpose.
- *Establish a post office.* Establish a post office in the classroom and provide students with opportunities to write, mail, and receive letters to and from their classmates and teacher.
- *Teach visualization.* Ask the students to close their eyes and visualize a paragraph that the teacher reads aloud. Another variation of this technique is to ask a student to describe a recent event while the other students close their eyes and visualize what is being said as a written paragraph.
- *Require students to proofread their own work.* Require that the students proofread their work before turning in written assignments. Provide the students with a list of items to check when proofreading their own work.

Spelling

To help students with LD who are poor spellers, the following techniques have been found to be helpful:

- *Use everyday examples of difficult spelling words.* Take advantage of everyday events to teach difficult spelling words in context. For example, ask a student eating a cheese sandwich to spell *sandwich*.

- *Assign frequently used words.* Assign spelling words that the student routinely uses in speech each day.
- *Have students keep a dictionary of misspelled words.* Ask the student to keep a personal dictionary of frequently misspelled words.
- *Use partner spelling activities.* Pair the student with another student. Ask the partners to quiz each other on the spelling of new words. Encourage both students to guess the correct spelling.
- *Use manipulatives.* Use cutout letters or other manipulatives to spell out hard-to-learn words.
- *Use color-coded letters.* Color code different letters in hard-to-spell words (e.g., *receipt*).
- *Use movement activities.* Combine movement activities with spelling lessons (e.g., jump rope while spelling words out loud).
- *Use word banks.* Write frequently misspelled words on 3" × 5" index cards and sort them alphabetically.

Handwriting

Students with LD who have difficulty with manuscript or cursive writing may benefit from their teacher's use of the following instructional practices:

- *Provide individual chalkboards.* Ask the student to practice copying and erasing the target words on a small, individual chalkboard. Two students can be paired to practice their target words together.
- *Provide quiet places for handwriting.* Provide the student with a special "quiet place" (e.g., a table outside the classroom) to complete handwriting assignments.
- *Teach spacing words on a page.* Teach the students to use a finger to measure how much space to leave between each word in a written assignment.
- *Have the student use special writing paper.* Ask the student to use special paper with vertical lines to learn to space letters and words on a page.

Math Computation

Numerous individualized instructional practices can help students with LD improve their basic computation skills. The following are just a few:

- *Teach students to recognize patterns in math.* Teach the student to recognize patterns when adding, subtracting, multiplying, or dividing whole numbers (e.g., the digits of numbers that are multiples of 9 [18, 27, 36, . . .] add up to 9).

- *Partner students for math activities.* Pair a student with LD with another student and provide opportunities for the partners to quiz each other about basic computation skills.
- *Review and be sure students understand math symbols.* If students do not understand the symbols used in math, they will not be able to do the work. For instance, do they understand that the *plus* in 1 + 3 means to add and that the *minus* in 5 – 3 means to take away?
- *Teach mnemonics for basic computation.* Teach the student mnemonics that describe basic steps in computing whole numbers. For example, "Don't miss Susie's boat" can be used to help the student recall the basic steps in long division (i.e., divide, multiply, subtract, and bring down).
- *Use real-life examples of money skills.* Provide the student with real-life opportunities to practice target money skills. For example, ask the student to calculate the change when paying for lunch in the school cafeteria, or set up a class store where students can practice calculating change.
- *Use color-coded arithmetic symbols.* Color code basic arithmetic symbols, such as +, –, and =, to provide visual cues for students when they are computing whole numbers.
- *Use calculators to check basic computation.* Ask the student to use a calculator to check addition, subtraction, multiplication, or division.
- *Provide board games to practice basic computation.* Ask the student to play board games to practice adding, subtracting, multiplying, and dividing whole numbers.
- *Schedule computer games to practice basic computation.* Schedule computer time for the student to drill and practice basic computations by playing appropriate games.
- *Have students perform "magic minute" drills.* Have students perform a quick (60-second) drill every day to practice basic computation of math facts, and have students track their own performance.

Solving Math Word Problems

To help students with LD improve their skill in solving word problems in mathematics, try the following:

- *Re-read the problem.* Teach the student to read a word problem *twice* before beginning to compute the answer.
- *Use clue words.* Teach the student clue words that identify which operation to use when solving word problems. For example,

words such as *sum, total,* or *all together* may indicate an addition operation.

- *Use guided questions for word problems.* Teach students to ask guiding questions in solving word problems. For example: What is the question asked in the problem? What information do you need to figure out the answer? What operation should you use to compute the answer?
- *Use real-life examples of word problems.* Ask the student to create and solve word problems that provide practice with specific target operations, such as addition, subtraction, multiplication, or division. These problems can be based on recent, real-life events in the student's life.
- *Allow calculators for students to check word problems.* Ask the student to use a calculator to check computations made in answering assigned word problems.

Use of Special Materials in Math

Some students with LD benefit from using special materials to help them complete their math assignments, including the following:

- *Number lines.* Provide number lines for the student to use when computing whole numbers.
- *Manipulatives.* Use manipulatives to help students gain basic computation skills. For example, the student might count poker chips when adding single-digit numbers.
- *Graph paper.* Ask the student to use graph paper to help organize columns when adding, subtracting, multiplying, or dividing whole numbers.

Organizational and Study Skills Useful for Academic Instruction of Students With LD

Many students with LD are easily distracted and have difficulty focusing their attention on assigned tasks. However, the following practices can help students with LD improve their organization of homework and other daily assignments:

- *Designate one teacher as the student's advisor or coordinator.* This teacher will regularly review the student's progress through progress reports submitted by other teachers and will act as the liaison between home and school. Permit the student to meet with this advisor on a regular basis (e.g., Monday morning) to plan and organize for the week and to review progress and problems from the past week.

- *Provide assignment notebooks.* Provide the student with an assignment notebook to help organize homework and other seatwork.
- *Use color-coded folders.* Provide the student with color-coded folders to help organize assignments for different academic subjects (e.g., reading, mathematics, social science, and science).
- *Assign students homework partners.* Assign the student a partner to help record homework and other seatwork in the assignment notebook and file worksheets and other papers in the proper folders.
- *Periodically have students clean out desks and book bags.* Ask the student periodically to sort through and clean out his or her desk, book bag, and other special places where written assignments are stored.
- *Use visual aids as reminders of subject material.* Use banners, charts, lists, pie graphs, and diagrams situated throughout the classroom to remind students of the subject material being learned.

Assisting Students With LD With Time Management

Students with LD often have difficulty finishing their assignments on time and can thus benefit from special materials and practices that help them to improve their time management skills. These include the following:

- *Use a clock or wristwatch.* Teach the student how to read and use a clock or wristwatch to manage time when completing assigned work.
- *Use a calendar.* Teach the student how to read and use a calendar to schedule assignments.
- *Practice sequencing activities.* Provide the student with supervised opportunities to break down a long assignment into a sequence of short, interrelated activities.
- *Create a daily activity schedule.* Tape a schedule of planned daily activities to the student's desk.

Helpful Study Skills for Students With LD

Students with LD often have difficulty in learning how to study effectively on their own. The following strategies may assist LD students in developing the study skills necessary for academic success:

- *Adapt worksheets.* Teach a student how to adapt instructional worksheets. For example, help a student fold the reading worksheet to reveal only one question at a time. The student can also use a blank piece of paper to cover the other questions on the page.

- *Teach students how to use Venn diagrams.* Teach a student how to use Venn diagrams to help illustrate and organize key concepts in reading, mathematics, or other academic subjects.
- *Teach note-taking skills.* Teach a student with LD how to take notes when organizing key academic concepts that have been learned, perhaps with the use of a program such as Anita Archer's Skills for School Success (Archer & Gleason, 2002).
- *Provide students with a checklist of frequent mistakes.* Provide the student with a checklist of mistakes that are frequently made in written assignments (e.g., punctuation or capitalization errors), mathematics (e.g., addition or subtraction errors), or other academic subjects. Teach the student how to use this list when proofreading work at home and school.
- *Provide students with a checklist of homework supplies.* Provide the student with a checklist that identifies categories of items needed for homework assignments (e.g., books, pencils, and homework assignment sheets).
- *Teach students about the importance of an uncluttered workspace.* Teach a student with LD how to prepare an uncluttered workspace to complete assignments. For example, instruct the student to clear away unnecessary books or other materials *before* beginning seatwork.
- *Track the progress of homework assignments.* Keep track of how well your students with LD complete their assigned homework. Discuss and resolve with them and their parents any problems in completing these assignments. For example, evaluate the difficulty of the assignments and how long the students spend on their homework each night. Keep in mind that the *quality*, rather than the *quantity*, of homework assigned is the most important issue. While doing homework is an important part of developing study skills, it should be used to reinforce skills and to review material learned in class, rather than to present, in advance, large amounts of material that is new to the student.

Behavioral Interventions

The second major component of effective instruction for students with LD involves the use of behavioral interventions. Students with LD often act immaturely, exhibiting behavior that resembles that of younger students, and have difficulty learning how to control their impulsiveness and hyperactivity. They may have problems forming friendships with other students in the class and may have difficulty thinking through the social consequences of their actions.

The purpose of behavioral interventions is to assist students in displaying the behaviors that are most conducive to their own learning and that of classmates. Well-managed classrooms prevent many disciplinary problems and provide an environment that is most favorable for learning. When a teacher's time must be spent interacting with students whose behaviors are not focused on the lesson being presented, less time is available for assisting other students. Behavioral interventions should be viewed as opportunities for teaching in the most effective and efficient manner rather than as opportunities for punishment.

Effective Behavioral Intervention Techniques

Effective teachers in the inclusion classroom use a number of behavioral intervention techniques to help students learn how to control their behavior. Perhaps the most important and effective of these is verbal reinforcement of appropriate behavior. The most common form of verbal reinforcement is praise that is given to a student when beginning and completing an activity or exhibiting a particular desired behavior. Simple phrases, such as "good job," encourage a student to act appropriately. Effective teachers praise students with LD frequently and look for a behavior to praise before, and not after, a student gets off-task.

The following strategies provide some guidance regarding the use of praise:

- *Define the appropriate behavior while giving praise.* Praise should be specific for the positive behavior displayed by the student: The comments should focus on what the student did right and should include exactly what part(s) of the student's behavior was desirable. Rather than praising a student for not disturbing the class, for example, a teacher should praise the student for quietly completing a math lesson on time.
- *Provide praise immediately.* The sooner that approval is given regarding appropriate behavior, the more likely the student will repeat it.
- *Vary the statements given as praise.* The comments used by teachers to praise appropriate behavior should vary; when students hear the same praise statement over and over, it may lose its value.
- *Be consistent and sincere with praise.* Appropriate behavior should receive consistent praise. Consistency among teachers with respect

to desired behavior is important to avoid confusion on the part of students with LD. Similarly, students will notice when teachers give insincere praise, and this insincerity will make praise less effective.

It is important to keep in mind that the most effective teachers focus their behavioral intervention strategies on *praise* rather than on *punishment.* Negative consequences may temporarily change behavior, but they rarely change attitudes and may actually increase the frequency and intensity of inappropriate behavior by rewarding misbehaving students with attention. Moreover, punishment may only teach students what not to do; it does not provide students with the skills that they need to do what is expected. Positive reinforcement produces the changes in attitudes that will shape a student's behavior over the long term.

In addition to verbal reinforcement, the following set of generalized behavioral intervention techniques has proven helpful with students with LD:

- *Selectively ignore inappropriate behavior.* It is sometimes helpful for teachers to ignore inappropriate behavior selectively. This technique is particularly useful when the behavior is unintentional or unlikely to recur or is intended solely to gain the attention of teachers or classmates but does not disrupt the classroom or interfere with the learning of others.
- *Remove nuisance items.* Teachers often find that certain objects (such as rubber bands and toys) distract the attention of students with LD. The removal of nuisance items is generally most effective after the student has been given the choice of putting it away immediately and then fails to do so.
- *Provide calming manipulatives.* While some toys and other objects can be distracting for both the students with LD and peers in the classroom, some students with LD can benefit from having access to objects that can be manipulated quietly. Manipulatives may help students gain some needed sensory input while still attending to the lesson.
- *Allow for "escape valve" outlets.* Permitting students with LD to leave class for a moment, perhaps on an errand (such as returning a book to the library), can be an effective means of settling them down and allowing them to return to the room ready to concentrate.
- *Provide activity reinforcement.* Students receive activity reinforcement when they are encouraged to perform a less desirable behavior before a preferred one.

- *Hold parent conferences.* Parents have a critical role in the education of students, and this axiom may be particularly true for those with LD. As such, parents must be included as partners in planning for the student's success. Partnering with parents entails including parental input in behavioral intervention strategies, maintaining frequent communication between parents and teachers, and collaborating in monitoring the student's progress.
- *Utilize peer mediation.* Members of a student's peer group can positively impact the behavior of students with LD. Many schools now have formalized peer mediation programs in which students receive training to manage disputes involving their classmates.

Effective teachers also use behavioral prompts with their students. These prompts remind students about expectations for their learning and behavior in the classroom. Three that may be particularly helpful are the following:

- *Visual cues.* Establish simple, nonintrusive visual cues to remind the student to remain on-task. For example, you can point at the student while looking him or her in the eye, or you can hold out your hand, palm down, near the student.
- *Proximity control.* When talking to a student, move to where the student is standing or sitting. Your physical proximity to the student will help the student to focus and pay attention to what you are saying.
- *Hand gestures.* Use hand signals to communicate privately with a student with LD. For example, ask the student to raise a hand every time you ask a question. A closed fist can signal that the student knows the answer; an open palm can signal that the student does not know the answer. You would call on the student to answer only when a fist is made.

In some instances, students with LD benefit from instruction designed to help students learn how to manage their own behavior:

- *Social skills classes.* Teach students with LD appropriate social skills using a structured class. For example, you can ask the students to role-play and model different solutions to common social problems. It is critical to provide for the generalization of these skills, including structured opportunities for the students to use the social skills that they learn. Offering such classes, or experiences, to the general school population can positively affect the school climate.

- *Problem-solving sessions.* Discuss how to resolve social conflicts. Conduct impromptu discussions with one student or with a small group of students where the conflict arises. In this setting, for example, ask two students who are arguing about a game to discuss how to settle their differences. Encourage the students to resolve their problem by talking to each other in a supervised setting.

For many students with LD, functional behavioral assessments and positive behavioral interventions and supports, including behavioral contracts and management plans, tangible rewards, or token economy systems, are helpful in teaching them how to manage their own behavior. Because students' individual needs are different, it is important for teachers, along with the family and other involved professionals, to evaluate whether these practices are appropriate for their classrooms. Examples of these techniques, along with steps to follow when using them, include the following:

- *Functional behavioral assessment (FBA).* FBA is a systematic process for describing problem behavior and identifying the environmental factors and surrounding events associated with it. The team that works closely with the student who is exhibiting problem behavior (1) observes the behavior and identifies and defines its problematic characteristics, (2) identifies which actions or events precede and follow the behavior, and (3) determines how often the behavior occurs. The results of the FBA should be used to develop an effective and efficient intervention and support plan (Gable et al., 1997).
- *Positive behavioral interventions and supports (PBIS).* This method is an application of a behaviorally based systems approach that is grounded in research regarding behavior in the context of the settings in which it occurs. Using this method, schools, families, and communities work to design effective environments to improve behavior. The goal of PBIS is to eliminate problem behavior, to replace it with more appropriate behavior, and to increase a person's skills and opportunities for an enhanced quality of life (Todd, Horner, Sugai, & Sprague, 1999).
- *Behavioral contracts and management plans.* Identify specific academic or behavioral goals for the student with LD, along with behavior that needs to change and strategies for responding to inappropriate behavior. Work with the student cooperatively to identify appropriate goals, such as completing homework assignments on time and obeying safety rules on the school playground. Take the time to ensure that the student agrees that goals are important to

master. Behavioral contracts and management plans are typically used with individual students, as opposed to entire classes, and should be prepared with input from parents.

- *Tangible rewards.* Use tangible rewards to reinforce appropriate behavior. These rewards can include stickers, such as happy faces or sports team emblems, or privileges, such as extra time on the computer or lunch with the teacher. Students should be involved in the selection of the reward. If students are invested in the reward, they are more likely to work for it.

- *Token economy systems.* Use token economy systems to motivate a student to achieve a goal identified in a behavioral contract. For example, a student can earn points for each homework assignment completed on time. In some cases, students also lose points for each homework assignment not completed on time. After earning a specified number of points, the student receives a tangible reward, such as extra time on a computer or a "free" period on Friday afternoon. Token economy systems are often used for entire classrooms as opposed to solely for individual students.

- *Self-management systems.* Train students to monitor and evaluate their own behavior without constant feedback from the teacher. In a typical self-management system, the teacher identifies behaviors that will be managed by a student and provides a written rating scale that includes the performance criteria for each rating. The teacher and student separately rate student behavior during an activity and compare ratings. The student earns points if the ratings match or are within one point of the teacher's and receives no points if ratings are more than one point apart; points are exchanged for privileges. With time, the teacher's involvement is removed, and the student becomes responsible for self-monitoring (DuPaul & Stoner, cited in Shinn, Walker, & Stoner, 2002).

Classroom Accommodations

The third component of a strategy for effectively educating students with LD involves physical classroom accommodations. Students with LD often have difficulty adjusting to the structured environment of a classroom, determining what is important, and focusing on their assigned work. They are easily distracted by other students or by nearby activities in the classroom. As a result, many students with LD benefit from accommodations that reduce distractions in the classroom environment and help them to stay on task and learn. Certain accommodations within the physical and learning environments of the classroom can benefit students with LD.

Special Classroom Seating Arrangements for LD Students

One of the most common accommodations that can be made to the physical environment of the classroom involves determining where a student with LD will sit. Three special seating assignments may be especially useful:

- *Seat the student near the teacher.* Assign the student a seat near your desk or the front of the room. This seating assignment provides opportunities for you to monitor and reinforce the student's on-task behavior.
- *Seat the student near a student role model.* Assign the student a seat near a student role model. This seat arrangement provides opportunity for students to work cooperatively and to learn from their peers in the class.
- *Provide low-distraction work areas.* As space permits, teachers should make available a quiet, distraction-free room or area for quiet study time and test taking. Students should be directed to this room or area privately and discreetly to avoid the appearance of punishment.

Instructional Tools and the Physical Learning Environment

Skilled teachers use special instructional tools to modify the classroom learning environment and accommodate the special needs of their students with LD. They also monitor the physical environment, keeping in mind the needs of these students. The following tools and techniques may be helpful:

- *Pointers.* Teach the student to use a pointer to visually track written words on a page. For example, provide the student with a bookmark to help the student follow along when students are taking turns reading aloud.
- *Egg timers.* Note for the students the time at which the lesson is starting and the time at which it will conclude. Set a timer to indicate to students how much time remains in the lesson and place the timer at the front of the classroom; the students can check the timer to see how much time remains. Interim prompts can be used as well. For instance, students can monitor their

own progress during a 30-minute lesson if the timer is set for 10 minutes three times.

- *Classroom lights.* Turning the classroom lights on and off prompts students that the noise level in the room is too high and they should be quiet. This practice can also be used to signal that it is time to begin preparing for the next lesson.
- *Music.* Play music on a tape recorder or chords on a piano to prompt students that they are too noisy. In addition, playing different types of music on a tape recorder communicates to students what level of activity is appropriate for a particular lesson. For example, play quiet classical music for quiet activities done independently and jazz for active group activities.
- *Proper use of furniture.* The desk and chair used by students with LD need to be the right size; if they are not, the student will be more inclined to squirm and fidget. A general rule of thumb is that students should be able to put their elbows on the surface of the desk and have their chin fit comfortably in the palm of the hand.

7

Promoting Positive Social Interactions in an Inclusion Setting

If you are working or going to work as either a general education or special education teacher in an inclusion classroom, you will be involved in a myriad of positive and challenging experiences. None of these will be more rewarding than helping children with special needs develop positive social interactions with their peers.

One of the components of successful inclusion is the degree to which the student with a disability feels a part of the general education classroom. Teachers may use many strategies to help the student achieve a sense of belonging to the class and school.

One of the most critical things an inclusion classroom teacher must do is establish and maintain a positive and supportive classroom atmosphere. Students are more likely to follow directions, work hard, and exhibit positive classroom behavior when they feel wanted and appreciated by the teacher. This may be especially true of particularly difficult students, who may not trust adults and who may feel that most teachers are "out to get them."

Review of Inclusion

What is inclusion? Inclusion involves keeping special education students in general education classrooms and bringing the support services to the child, rather than bringing the child to the support services.

Inclusion expresses commitment to educate each child, to the maximum extent appropriate, in the school and classroom that student would otherwise attend. It involves bringing the support services to the child (rather than moving the child to the services) and requires only that the child will benefit from being in the class (rather than requiring that the child keep up with the other students). Proponents of inclusion generally favor newer forms of education service delivery (Wisconsin Education Association Council, 2007).

The term *inclusion* does not appear in federal law or regulations, but its use to refer to the concept of integration of students with disabilities has become standard, and many court cases use the term. In the literature, one will encounter *inclusion, full inclusion, integration, full integration, inclusive schools, inclusive education,* and *unified system*—all terms used to describe the philosophy and the practices of the full participation of students with disabilities in regular education classrooms (Price, Mayfield, McFadden, & Marsh, 2001).

There seem to be two general approaches to inclusion: inclusion and full inclusion (Price et al., 2001).

1. Inclusion represents a belief that students with disabilities belong in regular programs of the school where special services are available to support the effort.

2. Full inclusion apparently has two variations:
   (a) Special education should be dismantled.
   (b) Special education should exist only in the regular classroom.

Full inclusion means that all students, regardless of handicapping condition or severity, will be in a regular classroom/program full time. All services must be taken to the child in that setting (Wisconsin Education Association Council, 2001).

Advocates of full inclusion are sometimes referred to disparagingly as "radical" inclusionists. These approaches form the boundaries of the debate about inclusion (Price et al., 2001).

Principles of Effective Inclusion

According to Salend (2001), there are four principles of effective inclusion:

1. Effective inclusion improves the educational system for all students by placing them together in general education classrooms regardless of their learning ability, race, linguistic ability, economic status, gender, learning style, ethnicity, cultural background, religion, family structure, and sexual orientation. Inclusionary schools welcome, acknowledge, affirm, and celebrate the value of all learners by educating them together in high-quality, age-appropriate general education classrooms in their neighborhood schools.

2. Effective inclusion involves sensitivity to and acceptance of individual needs and differences. Educators cannot teach students without taking into account the factors that shape students and make them unique. In inclusive classrooms, all students are valued as individuals capable of learning and contributing to society. They are taught to appreciate diversity and to value and learn from each other's similarities and differences.

3. Effective inclusion requires reflective educators to modify their attitudes, teaching and classroom management practices, and curricula to accommodate individual needs. In inclusive classrooms, teachers are reflective practitioners who are flexible, responsive, and aware of students' needs. They think critically about their values and beliefs and routinely examine their own practices for self-improvement and to ensure that all students' needs are met.

4. Effective inclusion is a group effort; it involves collaboration among educators, other professionals, students, families, and community agencies. The support and services that students need are provided in the general education classroom. People work cooperatively and reflectively, sharing resources, responsibilities, skills, decisions, and advocacy for students' benefit.

Why Are Social Skills Important?

Social competence is the degree to which students are able to establish and maintain satisfactory interpersonal relationships, gain peer acceptance, establish and maintain friendships, and terminate negative or pernicious interpersonal relationships. Effective social problem solving requires reading one's own and others' feelings and being able to label those feelings accurately and express them. Such skills are aspects of social and emotional learning (Zins et al., 1998, p. 19). Well-developed social skills can help youth with disabilities develop strong and positive peer relationships, succeed in school, and begin successfully to explore adult roles such as employee, coworker/colleague, and community member. Social skills also support the positive development of healthy adult relationships with family members and peers. Hair, Jager, and Garrett (2002) observe that adolescents who have strong social skills, particularly in the areas of conflict resolution, emotional intimacy, and the use of pro-social behaviors, are more likely to be accepted by peers, develop friendships, maintain stronger relationships with parents and peers, be viewed as effective problem solvers, cultivate greater interest in school, and perform better academically (p. 3). Adequate social skills need to be acquired while students are still enrolled in school and further supported and refined in postsecondary, community, and work settings.

Social-Cognitive Skill Development

Social relationships are an important aspect of the learning process and the classroom environment. Research has demonstrated that a significant proportion of students who fail to adjust socially to the classroom environment lack effective social-problem-solving skills. Social problems include the following:

- Poor ability to be empathetic to others' perspectives
- Poor impulse control
- Inability to generate multiple and effective solutions to problems faced in the classroom

Deficiencies in cognitive problem-solving skills often lead to emotional and behavioral disorders requiring treatment. The teacher in the inclusive classroom needs to address the social-behavioral domain as well as the academic domain. Research on teaching indicates giving training in social-cognitive skills to youth who are at risk of failure in general education classrooms can improve students' social effectiveness and achievement of social goals and reduce problem behaviors (Kochhar, West, & Taymans, 2000).

The Role of Social Skills at School

Gresham, Sugai, and Horner (2001) note that deficits in social skills are key criteria in defining many high-incidence disabilities that hinder students' academic progress, such as specific learning disabilities, attention deficit hyperactivity disorder (ADHD), mental retardation, and emotional disturbance (p. 332). Therefore, helping students learn social skills is a proactive approach to minimizing the impact of these disabilities on school success.

When social skills are absent, educators cannot fully engage students in a variety of learning experiences, especially those that are cooperative. As inclusion classroom teachers increasingly use cooperative learning strategies across their curricula, the need for students to have strong social skills is evident. To participate fully in cooperative learning, some students with disabilities need training in skills such as giving and receiving feedback, listening, and appropriate self-disclosure.

Strategies to Foster a Sense of Belonging in the Inclusion Classroom

Any teacher who has tried to improve a student's social skills knows there are significant challenges to such an endeavor. Problems that interfere with the effectiveness of social skill interventions may include oppositional behavior, conduct problems, negative influences from peer groups, substance abuse, family difficulties, and limited cognitive abilities (Hansen, Nangle, & Meyer, 1998).

Why would students want to improve their social skills? Most likely, they seek to (a) avoid the negative consequences of inadequate social skills, including loneliness, job loss, or embarrassment at school or work, and (b) enjoy the benefits of having good social skills, such as friendship, acceptance from others, and good relationships at school and work. Nonetheless, students must see the need for the skills being taught. In an inclusion classroom setting, teachers may ask students to identify the social skills necessary for achieving goals important to them. Based on such discussions, students and teachers can jointly select one or two skills to work on at a time.

A feeling of belonging positively affects the self-image and self-esteem of students with learning disabilities, as well as their motivation to achieve, speed of adjustment to the larger classroom and new demands, general behavior, and general level of achievement. The impact of the new student on the general classroom is a major consideration for inclusion planners. Fostering positive social relationships between students with disabilities and their peers requires the preparation of nondisabled peers in the classroom so that they understand the needs of their new classmates.

Strategies to foster a sense of belonging include the following (Kochhar et al., 2000):

- Discuss expectations with the student's peers and encourage interaction; the school counselor or psychologist can be helpful in preparing classes for a new student with a disability and in discussing the benefits of positive peer relationships.

- Use cooperative group learning, in which students are teamed for activities or projects and must cooperate, share ideas and materials, and share in the development of project products. Learning teams are also effective when students are required to prepare for classroom demonstrations and exhibitions.
- Assign a peer advocate, peer mentor, or "buddy" who is responsible for interacting with and helping the student in classroom activities and social situations. The peer advocate provides support and encouragement and enables the student with a disability to solve problems with class activities and generally adjust to the new classroom environment.
- Assign a teacher advocate to the student with whom the student can consult for guidance, general support, or crisis assistance.
- Include the new student in the daily roll call and in all class pictures, and place the student's work on the bulletin boards right along with the work of peers.
- Establish a lunch-buddy system (particularly helpful for younger students in the first weeks of class).

Creating a Positive Inclusion Classroom Climate

Consistent and effective use of acquired social skills is more likely to occur in inclusion classrooms having a positive social atmosphere. Most adults can think of a situation in which they didn't feel valued and, as a result, did not respond appropriately or compassionately to others. The inclusion classroom can ensure that all students know they are valued and respected members of a learning community by taking the following steps to create a positive school climate (Curtis, 2003):

- Learn and use students' names and know something about each student. This can be difficult in secondary schools; using name tags or assigned seating at the beginning of each term can be helpful.
- Hold daily classroom meetings each morning to help build a sense of community and provide opportunities for conversation among students.
- Provide unstructured time (e.g., recess) when students can practice their social skills with peers and experience feedback.
- Encourage journal writing to improve self-awareness.
- Provide opportunities for students to participate noncompetitively (without tryouts or auditions) in extracurricular activities. Avoid unnecessary competition among students.

- Provide ways for students to provide feedback regarding their experience at school and show them that their input is taken seriously.
- Make a point of connecting briefly and informally, over a period of several days, with individual students who are having difficulties. This establishes a relationship that will be helpful if the student's situation requires a more formal discussion at another time.

To be effective and worthwhile, social skills training must result in skills that (a) are socially relevant in the individual's life (social validity), (b) are used in a variety of situations (generalization), and (c) are maintained over time (treatment adherence; Hansen et al., 1998). Such skills will be most consistently employed in a setting that is supportive and respectful of each person's individuality.

Teaching Social Skills Through Role-Playing and Observation

Role-playing is a helpful technique for engaging student interest and providing opportunities for practice and feedback. One way to establish motivation and to inject some humor into the learning process is to ask students to role-play a situation in which the identified skill is lacking. Role-playing allows students to take on roles, provide feedback to one another, and practice new skills. Role-playing enables students to simulate a wide range of school, community, and workplace interactions. For students with intellectual disabilities, role-playing can provide an opportunity to practice appropriate small talk, a social skill that is key to acceptance in the inclusion classroom.

Role-playing exercises can help develop automaticity with small talk appropriate to the inclusion classroom. Following are some examples:

- Practicing automatic and brief responses for greetings and farewells. Responses should be brief, appropriate, and unelaborated. To "how" questions (e.g., "How are you doing?"), an appropriate response is "Fine," or "Great." To "what" questions (e.g., "What's up?"), an appropriate response is "Not much." The ability to use automatic and appropriate responses can be helpful in getting off to a good start in a new workplace.
- Practicing extending small talk by learning to add questions like "How about you?" or "What about you?" or "What have you been doing?" to the above responses.

- Role-playing an interaction that includes acting out social errors, spotting the errors, and correcting them in a subsequent role-play (with more able young adults). Examples of errors include bringing up inappropriate topics for small talk; making an inappropriately long response or, alternatively, no response when one is needed; making an inappropriately detailed response; and using a small-talk formula when it is not appropriate.

The Inclusion Classroom Teacher's Power to Model Acceptance

Research on inclusion has found that students who are appropriately placed into inclusive classrooms are more successful when their nondisabled peers are accepting and supportive. Many schools are establishing peer-mentor relationships to educate children without learning disabilities about the needs of their classmates with LD and help build relationships for emotional and social support. However, probably the most important influence on positive classroom relationships and social attitudes is the attitude of the teacher and the degree to which the teacher models acceptance of students with special needs. Inclusion classroom teachers must directly address the importance of mutual acceptance and support within the classroom, and they must reflect on their own attitudes and ability to demonstrate such acceptance (Kochhar et al., 2000).

Promoting Positive Interactions

Effective inclusion classroom teachers are distinguished by their positive approach to dealing with disciplinary problems. Rather than waiting for problems to develop and then reacting, effective inclusion classroom teachers organize their classrooms to promote positive behavior. Rather than looking for a quick fix for behavioral problems and issues, effective inclusion classroom teachers make a commitment to long-term behavioral change. This section will focus on strategies to promote positive social interactions among all students that effective inclusion classroom teachers can use in their everyday teaching and daily routine both in and outside of the classroom. Use the strategies discussed below along with the behavioral interventions described in Chapter 6 to facilitate interactions among students with and without disabilities.

Conduct Class Meetings

Students, as a group, can share their opinions and brainstorm solutions to class behavior problems, as well as general topics that concern them, during class meetings. Class meetings are designed to help students understand the perspectives of others, so they are especially effective for resolving conflicts between students based on cultural differences. Classroom problems and tensions between students in the inclusion classroom can be identified and handled by placing a box in the classroom where students and adults submit compliments and descriptions of problems and situations that made them feel upset, sad, annoyed, or angry. Compliments and concerns can be shared with the class, and all students can brainstorm possible solutions.

Use Values Clarification

Values clarification views classroom misbehavior as a result of confused values. Values clarification activities that are part of the curriculum allow students to examine their attitudes, interests, and feelings and learn how these values affect their behavior. For example, after students express their attitudes or opinions or use a specific behavior, you might ask them, "How did that affect you and others?" "Why is that important to you?" and "Did you consider any alternatives?" You can also use values clarification by creating a nonjudgmental, open, and trusting environment. Such an atmosphere encourages students to share their values, feelings, and beliefs and respect those of others (Salend, 2001).

Project a Feeling, Caring Persona

Convince students that you like them (even though you might not always like their behaviors). Take time to greet students at the door when they first arrive at the classroom. Address students by name and express an interest in their activities. Build up a store of positive comments to individual students, so that if later you must deliver negative feedback, it is not the first evaluation you have made of the student. Above all, try to assure students that you genuinely like them and that you have their best interests in mind. Even though you will have both positive and negative reactions to their specific behaviors, you nevertheless always value them as individuals.

Use Reprimands Judiciously

Although positive responses to positive behavior are among the best overall methods of classroom management, negative feedback in the form of reprimands is sometimes necessary to help students succeed in your classroom. Overall, reprimands are best viewed as direct feedback that the student's behavior is inappropriate. If they are provided in a way that indicates concern for the student's well-being, they can be effective in improving behavior. Reprimands are less effective when viewed as punishment—that is, that criticism and scorn or a negative, aggressive, or hostile tone of voice is expected to prevent the student from repeating the inappropriate behavior.

Research on reprimands suggests the following (Kerr & Nelson, 2002):

- Reprimand students privately, not publicly, to avoid humiliating or embarrassing them.
- Stand near the student you are reprimanding. This allows you to use a more confidential tone of voice. However, remaining one leg's length away respects the student's personal space.
- Use a normal tone of voice. Students can become desensitized over time to raised voices and may be less inclined to respond defensively to a calm tone.
- Look at the student while you are speaking, but do *not* insist that the student return your eye contact. Forced eye contact can be viewed as hostile and aggressive and, in some cases, even violate cultural norms.
- Never point your finger at the student you are reprimanding, as this again conveys aggression and hostility.
- Do not insist on having the last word. The final goal of your reprimand is increased compliance with class rules, not in getting the final word.

Validate Student Feelings

Sometimes when faced with a reprimand, students accuse teachers of unfair treatment. For example, a student might say, "It doesn't matter what I do—you are always picking on me!" This type of accusation often results in a defensive statement from the teacher: "I am not picking on you," or, "I treat everyone in this class the same."

Instead of making a defensive comment, try validating the student's feelings by asking for specifics: "I really don't want you to think I am picking on you. If you give me specific examples, maybe we can solve the problem." Such an approach not only avoids a confrontation, it also validates the student's expressed feeling (whether "true" or not), as well as subtly challenging the student to document "always" being picked on. It also openly attempts to keep the lines of communication open.

Post Positive Behavior

Public posting of students' behaviors has also been seen to reduce behavior problems. Students' behaviors can be evaluated and recorded on publicly posted charts. Students who follow classroom rules can be given a star next to their name for each class period, day, or other appropriate length of time.

Promote Self-Monitoring

Self-monitoring strategies involve teaching students to monitor and evaluate their own classroom behavior. In some cases, students may be asked to monitor their general on-task behavior. In other cases, students may monitor themselves for a specific behavior, such as teasing. Before implementing self-monitoring interventions, meet individually and discuss with students the purpose and importance of classroom behavior and how they will benefit personally from better classroom behavior. The students should be made to understand that the intervention is in their best interest.

Train for Generalization

Most positive social behaviors are of limited use unless they can be shown to generalize to appropriate situations outside the training context. It is particularly important that students in inclusive settings are able to generalize all the positive social behaviors they have learned in other settings; however, students with special needs often demonstrate problems in generalizing learned behavior. As important social behaviors are learned, make a list of all the settings and situations into which behavior must generalize and all the individuals who will observe the generalized behavior. Then create a plan to promote generalization across all these settings and individuals.

Deal Appropriately With Name-Calling and Teasing

Friendships in classrooms and positive behavior can be established by preventing name-calling and teasing or stopping these behaviors as soon as they happen. Effective behavioral management for these situations includes the following:

- Establishing a rule about no name-calling and teasing
- Making it clear to students that name-calling and teasing will not be tolerated
- Responding immediately to incidents of name-calling and teasing with a discussion of differences and discrimination
- Helping students to recognize and explore the reasons why they are uncomfortable with individual differences
- Helping students to understand individual differences by giving them information

Offer Choices and Solicit Preferences

Allowing students to make choices and express their preferences can promote self-determination. Because the school day involves a series of choices, you can integrate activities involving choices into both teaching and nonteaching parts of the daily schedule. If students have difficulty making choices, you can start by providing them with options. Cooperative learning arrangements, student-selected projects and rewards, self-management and metacognitive techniques, and learning strategies also allow students to guide their own learning.

Promote Self-Esteem

Promoting self-esteem in students can improve their ability to advocate for themselves. Students with low self-esteem often make negative statements about themselves that hinder their performance, such as "I'm not good at this, and I'll never complete it." You can promote self-esteem by helping students understand the harmful effects of low self-esteem and by structuring academic and social situations so that students succeed. Other methods include recognizing students' achievements and talents, teaching them to use self-management techniques, asking them to perform meaningful classroom and school-based jobs, and posting their work in the classroom and throughout the school.

Provide Attribution Training

Students' self-determination and self-esteem can be fostered by attribution training, which involves teaching students to analyze the events and actions that lead to both success and failure. Students who understand attribution recognize and acknowledge that their positive performance is due to effort and other factors within themselves. Students who fail to understand attribution often attribute their poor performance to bad luck, teacher error, lack of ability, or other external factors.

Demonstrate or Model Rules and Procedures; Then Allow Students to Rehearse Them

The teacher demonstrates both the correct and incorrect forms of the behavior (e.g., sitting at a desk quietly, getting to the pencil sharpener). The demonstration enables the students to discriminate the dimensions of the behavior. Students are then given an opportunity to practice the required behavior. Mastering rules and procedures is similar to learning academics; it requires teacher instruction and feedback combined with student practice.

After a student has received negative attention, provide immediate reinforcement and attention when the student displays the appropriate behavior. This identifies the accepted behavior and reaffirms that appropriate behaviors are reinforced and inappropriate behaviors are punished.

With Older Students, Use Contingency Contracts

Contingency contracts are written agreements between the teacher and the student that indicate what the student must do to earn a specific reward. These agreements, like most contracts, are negotiated; both parties must accept the terms. Because they involve negotiation and require students to assume responsibility for fulfilling their part of the bargain, contracts are probably best for older students.

Research suggests the following rules for developing contingency contracts with students in the classroom are effective:

- The initial contract payoff (reward) should be immediate.
- The initial contracts should call for and reward small approximations of the desired behavior.
- Reward frequently with small amounts.
- The contract should call for and reward accomplishment rather than obedience.
- Reward the behavior after it occurs.
- The contract must be fair.
- The terms of the contract must be clear.
- The contract must be honest.
- The contract must be positive.
- Contracting as a method must be used systematically.

In sum, a good contract identifies the responsibilities of both parties and the consequences if the terms are not fulfilled.

8

IEP Development and Educational Placement Options for Students With Learning Disabilities

According to IDEA 2004, every public school district is required to have an individualized education program (IEP) committee, which may be referred to as the "eligibility committee," "committee on special education," and so forth. If the population of students with special needs reaches a certain level, then more than one IEP committee may be formed. IEP committees are responsible for the identification of children with disabilities within the district and the recommendation of appropriate education at public expense for those students.

Members of the IEP Committee

The IEP committee is usually made up of members mandated by IDEA 2004 and assigned members whom the board of education deems necessary. Most states require that certain professionals and individuals be core members. Consistent with IDEA 2004, these members must include the following:

- The parent of, or person in a parental relationship to, the child with a disability
- A general education teacher of the child, if the child is or may be participating in the general education environment
- A special education teacher of the child or, if appropriate, a special education provider of the child
- A school psychologist
- A representative of the school district who is qualified to provide or supervise the provision of special education and is knowledgeable about the general curriculum and the availability of resources of the district. This individual can also be the special education teacher, the special education provider, or the school psychologist, provided he or she meets the other qualifications.
- An individual who can interpret the instructional implications of evaluation results. This individual can also be the general education teacher, the special education teacher, the special education provider, the school psychologist, a direct representative, or a person having knowledge or special expertise regarding the student if that person is determined by the district to have knowledge and expertise to fulfill this role.
- The student, where appropriate
- A school physician, if requested in writing by the student's parent or the district at least 72 hours prior to the meeting
- An additional parent member who is a parent of a student with a disability residing in the district or a neighboring district. However, the participation of this member is not required if the student's parents request that this additional parent member not participate in the meeting.
- At the discretion of the parent or the district, other individuals who have knowledge and special expertise regarding the student, including related services personnel, as appropriate

Responsibilities of the IEP Committee

The IEP committee is charged with many important responsibilities both before and after a child is classified in special education. Following are some of the responsibilities of IEP committee.

During the Initial Eligibility Meeting

- Following appropriate procedures and taking appropriate action for a child referred as having a suspected disability

- Determining the suitable classification for a child with a suspected disability
- Reviewing and evaluating all relevant information that may appear on each student with a disability
- Determining the least restrictive environment for any child having been classified as having a disability
- Finalizing the child's IEP

After the Child Is Classified

- Reviewing, at least annually, the status of the child (The annual review is discussed later in this chapter.)
- Evaluating the adequacy of programs, services, and facilities for the child
- Maintaining ongoing communication in writing to parents in regard to planning, modifying, changing, reviewing, placing, or evaluating the program, classification, or educational plan of the child
- Advising the board of education as to the status and recommendations of the child
- Making sure that every three years, the child is retested with a full educational and psychological battery. (The triennial review is discussed later in this chapter.)

Most IEP committees try to remain as informal as possible to reduce the anxiety of the situation. This is a crucial issue, because a parent entering a room with numerous professionals may feel overwhelmed or intimidated.

The parent member usually serves as a liaison and advocate for the parent(s), establishing contact prior to the meeting to reduce anxiety and alleviate any concerns that the parent(s) may have. School personnel should also be in contact with the parent(s) prior to the meeting to go over the process, their rights, and what may take place at the meeting. At no time should anyone in contact with the parent(s) prior to the meeting give false hope, make promises, or second-guess the IEP committee.

What needs to be communicated are procedural issues and options and the awareness that the IEP committee will make the recommendation, not one individual. Further, the parent(s) must be made aware of their rights; in particular, the liaison should make sure they understand their right to due process if they do not agree with the IEP committee's recommendations. Making sure parents understand their rights before the meeting may reduce the possibility of conflict.

IDEA 2004 and IEP Committee Meetings: What to Know

The reauthorized IDEA 2004 made clear that parents have a right to participate in IEP committee meetings with respect to the identification, evaluation, educational placement, and the provision of Free and Appropriate Public Education (FAPE) for their child.

IDEA 2004 regulations provide that a meeting does not include informal or unscheduled conversations involving school district personnel and conversations on issues such as teaching methodology, lesson plans, or coordination of service provision if those issues are not addressed in the child's IEP.

IDEA 2004 regulations also provide that if neither parent can participate in a meeting in which a decision is to be made relating to the educational placement of their child, the school district must use other methods to ensure their participation, including individual conference calls or videoconferencing.

The IEP committee may make a placement decision without the parent's participation in the decision, but in such an instance, the school district must have a record of its attempt to ensure the parent's involvement that includes the following information:

- Detailed records of telephone calls made or attempted and the results of those calls
- Copies of correspondence sent to the parent(s) and any responses received
- Detailed records of visits made to the parental home or place of employment and the results of those visits

IDEA 2004 regulations further require that school districts inform parents of the purpose of an IEP meeting, who will attend the meeting, and the time and location of the meeting. The regulations also indicate that it may be appropriate for a school district to ask the parents to inform it of any individuals the parents will be bringing to an IEP meeting and encourage parents to bring persons they feel may be helpful to them.

Development of the Information Packet for Presentation to the IEP Committee

Once the multidisciplinary team (MDT) has considered all the information and completed the evaluations, intakes, assessments, and so on, team members need to prepare the necessary information packet that will be presented to the district's IEP committee for review. This information will be viewed by all the members of the IEP committee along with the parents and other individuals so designated, such as an advocate or lawyer. This packet is a crucial part of the special education process, because most of the committee members will not be familiar with the child. They will use this information to determine the child's educational future. Therefore, it is imperative that the MDT present the most thorough and practical information to the committee.

To facilitate this process of preparing the required documentation for presentation, the team usually designates a case manager, the specific individual whose responsibility is to gather, organize, and forward the packet to the IEP committee. The case manager can be anyone, but in many cases, it will be either the special education teacher or the psychologist. All districts have their own specific forms and guidelines for presentation to the committee. However, in most cases, the information presented, regardless of the format, is similar.

This section presents an example of what information and documentation the case manager may need to forward to the IEP committee. It is a typical list of materials included in the eligibility packet that might be required by the committee for a review of a student for classification. Again, these materials vary from district to district and from state to state.

Required Forms

- *Initial referral to the MDT from school staff:* The child study team (CST) fills out this form when the team suspects that the child being reviewed may have an educational disability. This referral occurs when a child is being assessed for special education by the MDT for the first time; it usually involves children in general education who have had no prior services.
- *Initial referral to MDT from parent/guardian:* This form is filled out if the parent makes the initial referral for assessment to the MDT for a suspected disability, according to the parent's due process rights.
- *Assessment plan and parent consent:* This plan and form must be signed and dated by a parent prior to evaluation; it is part of the parent's due process rights.
- *Social history form:* This form provides the most recent pertinent background information on the child.
- *Medical report form:* Usually filled out by the teacher or school nurse, this includes medical information on the child from the last year that may be related to the child's learning problems.

- *Classroom observation form:* This form is the result of an on-site visit observation by some member of the CST.

Evaluations (Initial Referral)

- *Psychological:* A full psychological evaluation, including all identifying data, reason for referral, background and developmental history, prior testing results, observations, tests administered, test results (including a breakdown of scaled scores), conclusions, and recommendations, is required. This evaluation must be conducted within one year of the IEP committee meeting. It may also be helpful to include any prior evaluations done over the years.
- *Educational:* An educational evaluation, including identifying data, reason for referral, academic history, prior testing results, observations, tests administered, test results, conclusions, and recommendations, is required. This report should identify achievement strengths and weaknesses.
- *Speech/language:* A speech/language evaluation, including identifying data, reason for referral, observations, tests administered, test results, conclusions, and recommendations, should be included if applicable. A description of the severity of the language deficit should also be included and, if possible, the prognosis.
- *Vocational (secondary level only):* A copy of the child's Differential Aptitude Test results or other measures of vocational aptitude should be included, if applicable.
- *Other (e.g., occupational therapist, physical therapist, ESL, reading):* From time to time, parents or the school will have a variety of reports from outside agencies, such as medical, neurological, psychiatric, occupational therapy screening, physical therapy screening, psychological, audiological, visual training, and so forth. These reports should be included only when they are relevant to the possible disability. If outside reports are to be used in lieu of the district's own evaluations, they should be fairly recent, from within the past six months to one year.

Guidance and School Materials (Initial Referral)

- *Child's schedule:* This is a copy of the student's daily school schedule.
- *Transcript of past grades:* All the child's report card grades should be attached as far back as possible, or a report indicating the patterns of grades throughout the child's school career should be included.
- *Latest report card:* The most up-to-date report card should be included.

- *Teacher's reports:* Teacher reports in behavioral terms should be included from all the child's teachers.
- *Standardized achievement test scores:* Many schools require standardized achievement testing in certain grades. Any and all scores should be provided to reinforce historical patterns or levels of ability.
- *Discipline information:* Any referrals to the principal, dean, and so on should be included, as well as descriptions of incidents and disposition.
- *CST-related documents (i.e., minutes):* These provide the IEP committee with pertinent information regarding prior intervention strategies and procedures followed prior to the referral.
- *Attendance records:* Attendance patterns and records should be provided, especially if lack of attendance is a recurring issue and a serious symptom.

Other Materials

Some schools also may include the following materials in a draft form. The drafts become a working model at the IEP committee meeting, and the final version is mailed to the parent after the meeting. These materials may include the following:

- *Social, physical, academic, management (SPAM) needs:* In some states and school districts, a working draft copy of the child's needs should be included in the eligibility packet. These needs will provide the committee with an idea of the environmental, educational, social, and physical requirements under which the child may learn best.
- *Draft IEP, including goals and objectives:* In some states and school districts, a working draft copy of the IEP is prepared prior to the eligibility meeting. This is a basic working draft of the IEP, not the final draft, because no IEP can be finalized without parental involvement.
- *Testing modifications worksheet:* This worksheet outlines the suggested test and classroom modifications being suggested and the supporting data for such recommendations. As will be discussed, testing modifications are a component of the child's IEP. The modifications must be consistent with the criteria established. The worksheet may be completed by a member of the MDT or school staff to be processed as a draft recommendation for discussion at the IEP committee meeting.

o Depending on the state, there are usually four circumstances in which students with disabilities may be eligible to receive test modifications:

1. Students with disabilities whose individualized education program includes test modifications

2. Students who are declassified by the IEP committee

3. Students with disabilities whose Section 504 accommodation plan includes test modifications (Section 504 is a civil rights law, separate from IDEA, that prohibits discrimination against individuals with disabilities.)

4. Students who acquire disabilities shortly before test administration

In making its decision regarding the need for test modifications, the EC reviews all available information regarding the student's individual needs. Such information might include recent evaluations, previous school records and IEPs, classroom observations, and the student's experience on previous tests. Information and suggestions from the student's teachers, related service providers, and parents should also be sought. Testing modifications are to be limited to specific needs of the student.

If such a determination is made by the IEP committee and documented in the recommendation for declassification, the test modification(s) must continue to be provided consistently to the student for the balance of the student's public school education. The continuation of test modifications upon declassification, however, is not automatic. During subsequent school years, if it is felt that such modification(s) is no longer appropriate, the school staff is to meet with the student's parent to review and document the discontinuation or revision of the test modification(s).

The school principal may modify testing procedures for general education students who experience temporary (e.g., broken arm) or long-term (e.g., paraplegic) disabilities shortly before the administration of state exams, when sufficient time is not available for the development of an IEP or 504 plan. Also, if the student is expected to continue to need test modifications, the principal should make the appropriate referral for the development of an IEP or 504 plan.

- *Extended school year worksheet:* This worksheet provides the IEP committee with the information and criteria necessary to make a recommendation for extended school services in July and August.

At annual review meetings, parents of students with disabilities may ask for special education services during the summer (extended school year).

- *Extended school year criteria:* Depending on the state, the law may indicate the extended school year service be considered by the IEP committee when a student experiences substantial regression. *Substantial regression* means a student's inability to maintain developmental levels due to a loss of skill or knowledge during the months of July and August of such severity as to require an inordinate period of review at the beginning of the school year to reestablish and maintain IEP goals and objectives mastered at the end of the previous school year. For example, a teacher would project November 1 of the upcoming school year as the target date for the student to reacquire skills demonstrated at the end of the previous school year (a typical period of review or reteaching is up to 40 school days). Classroom teachers and/or service providers are expected to provide documentation (qualitative and/or quantitative) as to the evidence of regression for discussion at the IEP committee meeting.

An analysis of a student's substantial regression, if any, may be monitored during school vacation periods (winter, spring, summer). Note that the above definition includes not only regression but also an inordinate period of time to re-establish and maintain IEP goals/objectives. Extended school year services are not provided for students to improve their skills. Such instruction is a parent responsibility.

Extended year services may differ from services provided during the school year. The IEP committee will determine the type, amount, and duration of services to be provided. Extended school year services may be provided at a different location from where services are provided during the school year.

- *Adaptive physical education worksheet:* If a child's disability prevents the student from participating in the general education physical education program, then the district must provide adaptive alternatives that capitalize on the student's abilities. This worksheet outlines the criteria exhibited by the child for possible adaptive physical education. The behaviors, supporting reports, and data are included for the IEP committee to make a recommendation. The physical education teacher, in consultation with other IEP committee staff members, usually completes this. This worksheet then becomes a draft recommendation for discussion at the IEP committee meeting.
- *Other:* Information not noted in the above categories may also be provided to the IEP committee.

In conclusion, the above forms and information represent a picture of the child with a disability, including strengths, weaknesses, recommendations, and any other information that will assist the IEP committee in making the most educationally sound decision.

How Recommendations for Classification Are Made by the IEP Committee

In developing recommendations, all members of the eligibility committee (EC) discuss the evaluations presented and any other pertinent information on the child. The first issue to be decided is whether the child has an educational disability that adversely affects his or her educational performance. The EC will review the IEP committee packet prepared by the school and ask any sitting member pertinent questions necessary to clarify the information. If indicated by the evidence, the child will be classified according to the categories outlined in IDEA 2004.

The concept of least restrictive education (LRE) applies to the placement of students with disabilities in the most advantageous educational placement suitable for their needs. Contrary to the belief of many teachers and parents, LRE does not mean that every student with a disability must be placed in a regular classroom.

Specific Educational Placement (LRE) Considerations According to IDEA 2004

A *placement* is the location where the special educational program will be provided. According to IDEA 2004, the requirements involving least restrictive environment are the following:

- In selecting the LRE for a student with a disability, school districts must consider any potential harmful effect on the child or on the quality of services that the child needs.
- School districts may not remove a student with a disability from education in age-appropriate regular classrooms solely because of needed modifications in the general curriculum.
- LRE requirements apply to both nonacademic and extracurricular activities, including meals and recess periods, athletics, transportation, health services, recreational activities, special interest groups or school-sponsored clubs, and referrals to agencies that provide assistance to individuals with disabilities and employment

of students, including both employment by a public agency and assistance in making outside employment available.

IDEA 2004 regulations also indicate the following:

- The determination of an appropriate placement for a child whose behavior is interfering with the education of others requires careful consideration of whether the child could appropriately function in the regular classroom if appropriate behavioral supports, strategies, and interventions were provided.
- If a student's behavior in the regular classroom, even with the provision of appropriate behavioral supports, strategies, and interventions, would significantly impair the learning of others, that placement would not meet the child's needs and would not be appropriate for that child.

The placement of students with disabilities is the responsibility of the IEP committee with the input of staff and parents and final consent by the parents. The committee must analyze all available information and determine the best "starting placement" for the child that will ensure success and provide the child with the highest level of stimulation and experience for the child's specific disability and profile of strengths and weaknesses.

To accomplish this task, the IEP committee has a variety of placements from which to choose. These range in levels of restriction, including class size, student-teacher ratio, length of program, and the degree to which the child will be included in the general education population. In the normal course of events, it is hoped that children should be placed in a more restrictive environment only if it is to their educational advantage. In these cases, however, they should be moved to a less restrictive setting as soon as they are capable of being educated in that environment.

The placements below follow a path from least restrictive to most restrictive (Gargiulo, 2004):

General education classroom: General education class placement is the least restrictive placement for all children. This placement alone, without some type of special education supportive services, is not suitable for a child with a disability and is usually considered unsuitable by the IEP committee.

Inclusion classroom: Various models of inclusion classrooms are available as options in special education. Use of these models can vary from state to state and even district to district. In many instances, inclusion classroom placement involves including the child in a general education classroom assisted by the presence of a second teacher who is certified in special education.

General education class placement with consulting teacher assistance: A consultant teacher model is used when supportive special education services are required but the IEP committee feels that the child will be better served by remaining in the classroom rather than being pulled out for services. Because the child remains within the class, even though he or she is receiving services, this placement is considered the next least restrictive setting.

General education class placement with some supportive services: Regular class placement with supportive services may be used for students with mild disabilities who require supportive services but can remain in the regular class for the majority of the day. The services that may be provided at this level include adaptive physical education, speech and language therapy, in-school individual or group counseling, physical therapy, and occupational therapy.

General education class placement with itinerant specialist assistance: Itinerant services are services subcontracted by the district and provided by outside agencies. These services are usually provided for students when the disability is such that the district wishes to maintain the child in the district but an insufficient number of students with that disability attend school within the district to warrant hiring a teacher. An example of this situation might be a hard-of-hearing child who can maintain a regular class placement as long as supportive itinerant services by a teacher specializing in hearing impairments are provided.

General education class placement with resource room assistance: A resource room program is usually provided for students who need supportive services but can remain successfully within the regular classroom for the majority of the day. This type of program is a "pullout" program, and the services are usually provided in a separate room. The student-teacher ratio with this type of service is usually 5:1, and the amount of time spent within the resource room cannot exceed 50 percent of the child's day.

Part-time general education class placement: Part-time placement is for students who need a more restrictive setting for learning, behavioral, or intellectual reasons and cannot be successful in a full-time regular class or with a pullout supportive service but who can be included successfully in general education classroom for a part of the school day.

General education full-time special class in a general education school: A full-time special class in a regular school placement is viewed as the least restrictive setting for students whose disability does not permit successful participation in any type of regular class setting, even for part of the day. The students in a special class usually require a program that is very structured and closely monitored on a daily basis but not so restrictive as to warrant an out-of-district placement. These students can handle the rules and structure of a regular school building but not the freedom or style of a less restrictive setting within the school.

Special day school outside the school district: A special day school is a type of restrictive educational setting that is a desirable placement for students whose disability is so severe that they require a more thera-peutic environment and closer monitoring by specially trained special education teachers or staff members. The child is transported by dis-trict expense to the placement, and many state policies try to limit travel time on the bus to no more than one hour. These types of programs may have student-teacher-aide ratios of 6:1:1, 6:1:2, 9:1:1, 9:1:2, 12:1:1, or 15:1:1, depending upon the severity of the child's dis-ability. The more severe the disability, the lower the student-teacher ratio. These programs can run 10 or 12 months, again depending upon the severity of the disability and the individual needs of the child.

Residential school: Residential school placements are considered the next most restrictive placement. Not only do students with disabili-ties receive their education within this setting, but they also usually reside there for the school term. The nature and length of home vis-its depend on several factors that are usually determined by the residential school staff after evaluation and observation. For some students, home visits may not take place at all, whereas others may go home every weekend. Some students are placed in residential placements by the court. In this case, the child's local school district is only responsible for the costs of the educational portion, including related services if needed.

Homebound instruction: Homebound instruction provides a very restrictive setting, usually for students who are in the process of tran-sition between programs and have yet to be placed. It should never be used as a long-term placement because of the social restrictions and limitations. This option is also used when children are restricted to their house because of an illness, injury, and so on and this option remains the only realistic educational service until they recover. Homebound instruction requires an adult to be at home when the teacher arrives, or it can be held at a community center, library, or some other site deemed appropriate by the IEP committee.

Hospital or institution: The most restrictive setting used is a hospital or institution. Although this is the most restrictive setting, it may be the least restrictive possible setting for certain students, such as situations where an adolescent has attempted suicide or when a child has pervasive clinical depression or severe or profound retardation.

In conclusion, the least restrictive environment cannot be etched in concrete for an individual child. It is normally reviewed every year at the annual review, and a change can be made in either direction should the situation warrant it.

Once the IEP committee determines the most suitable LRE, committee members need to determine the facility or program that best fits the decision. The following examples are types of placements that the IEP committee may consider for the LRE in order of educational restriction:

Local school district: The child's home school of the local school district, depending on the severity of the disability, will generally provide the required services. This is often the preferred setting for the many reasons previously discussed. Maintaining the child in the child's home school should be the parents' and the district's goal. This, of course, is not always possible. If not, the next step is another school in the district.

Neighboring school district: Due to the nature of special education programs, all special education services are not offered within every district. The child's local school may arrange for participation in necessary programs and services in neighboring school districts if they cannot be provided within the child's home district.

Cooperative educational services: Cooperative educational service agencies are usually set up by your state to assist local districts with a student population or specific services one or more districts could not provide themselves.

Home/hospital settings: At times, a child may need temporary instruction at home or in a hospital setting due to severe illness or special circumstances indicated on the IEP. The key word here is *temporary.* The instruction should approximate what is offered in school within reasonable limits. Home and hospital instruction is highly restrictive; the continuing need for such services should be assessed frequently, and this service should be seen as temporary. State laws may vary as to the minimum amount of educational time allotted to children involved in these services. A general guide should be two hours per day of individual instruction for a secondary student and one hour per day for an elementary-grade student.

Private approved schools: School districts may place students in private schools, special act schools (schools set up by the state to provide services for a child with a disability), or residential placements approved by the state's education department. These private approved schools may be located in or out of state. Such placements are appropriate for students whom the home school district cannot service due to the severity and/or diversity of their medical, physical, mental, or emotional needs.

State-operated schools for the deaf, blind, and severely emotionally disturbed: These state-operated schools are examples of educational programs that are available for students with educational needs who require a school with a special focus.

It is the responsibility of the IEP committee to provide programs based on the least restrictive environment concept. Remember, it is important to provide programs that are in close proximity to the child's home (some states limit this to one hour on the bus). The child should have involvement with peers without disabilities. Finally, the program must be based on the student's needs.

When considering any of the above placements, everyone works toward providing the best possible placement for the child in the least restrictive environment. However, the school district needs to provide only an appropriate placement, not the best placement, in a program that is appropriate to the child's needs as close to home as possible.

Appealing the Decision of the IEP Committee

Identifying and finding an appropriate educational placement for a child with a disability should be a joint process between the district and the family. Assuming that the parents agree with the IEP committee's decisions, the parents will sign off on the IEP, and the child's program will begin as of the start date mandated in the IEP. When both the parents and the IEP committee work in the best interests of the child, the process can be very positive and rewarding. However, sometimes the family and the district disagree. When this occurs, the parents or the school has the right to due process. This procedure protects the rights of both the school and the family and allows for another avenue for resolution.

An impartial hearing officer may be requested to intervene when there is a difference of opinion. This is an independent individual assigned by the district's board of education or commissioner of education to hear an appeal and render a decision. Impartial hearing officers can in no way be connected to the school district, may have to be certified (depending upon state regulations), are trained, and usually must keep their skills updated.

Although due process rights of parents to continue this appeal to the state's department of education exist, if they disagree with the impartial hearing officer's decision, it is hoped that through a thorough understanding of the needs of the parent and the child, conflict resolution, and a positive working relationship, a solution that is acceptable to both sides can be established at the local level.

Other Roles of the IEP Committee

Special Meetings

Sometimes, the parents or IEP committee call a special meeting. This type of review can occur for several reasons and is always held for a child who has been previously classified. Among the reasons for such a meeting are the following:

- Change in a child's IEP
- Change in a child's educational placement
- Addition or deletion of a modification
- Parental request for an IEP committee meeting
- Disciplinary concerns
- New student to district previously identified as disabled
- Referral from the building administrator

Annual Review

Each year, the IEP committee is required to review the existing program of a child with a disability. Annual review meetings are required for all students receiving special instruction and/or related services. The required IEP committee participants in an annual review meeting may include the committee chairperson, psychologist, special education teacher, general education teacher (if student is in general education or will receive general education services), parent of child, parent member, and student (if over 16 years of age). During this process, the IEP committee will make recommendations based upon a review of the evidence that will continue, change, revise, or end the child's special education program. The IEP committee will make adjustments to the IEP and recommendations to the board of education.

The annual review occurs within a year of initial placement and yearly thereafter. The date of the annual review should be part of the child's IEP. However, a parent, the child's teacher, or a school administrator may request an IEP committee review at any time to determine if a change in placement is needed. If this occurs, the next review must be conducted within one year.

The parents are notified of the date, time, location, and individuals expected to attend their child's meeting. They will also be given a statement about their right to bring other people to the meeting. Parents have the same rights as at the initial IEP committee meeting, outlined above. They are also notified that if they cannot attend the meeting, they will have the opportunity to participate in other ways, such as through telephone calls or written reports of the annual review meeting. If necessary, they can have an interpreter provided at no cost to them. The parents' notice of their child's annual review includes their right to have information about the planned review: They may at any time inspect their child's school files, records, and reports and make copies at a reasonable cost. If medication or a physical condition is part of the child's disability, the parent may request that a physician attend the meeting. The parent may also request an independent evaluation, an impartial hearing, or an appeal of the decision from the impartial hearing to the state review office of the state's education department.

In some cases, the parent may be entitled to receive free or low-cost legal services and a listing of where those services can be obtained. Parents also are entitled to having the child stay in the current educational placement during formal due process proceedings, unless both parties agree otherwise.

After the annual review, the parents receive another notice regarding the recommendation that has been made to the board of education. A copy of their child's IEP is sent to them, indicating that their child has been recommended to continue to receive special education. The notice also explains all factors used to make the recommendation. Again, the notice describes the parents' due process rights.

Suggestions for the Special Educator's Participation in the Annual Review

When you attend an annual review meeting as a special educator, there are some key points that you should follow:

- Suggest ways to meet the child's proposed goals and objectives as specified in the IEP.
- Discuss changes or additions for the child's upcoming program and services. Talk about what worked and what needs adjustment from your point of view.
- Present the areas in which the child showed success and significant progress.
- Discuss high school diploma and credential options, if applicable.
- Discuss the need for a referral to an adult service provider—that is, state vocational rehabilitation coordinator—for services the child may need as an adult, if applicable.
- Review problems that the child has experienced or encountered throughout the year with the IEP committee and parent.
- When the child is 13, you should begin to consider plans for occupational education and transition services and become very familiar with the transitional process and all the factors involved.

Triennial Review

A child in special education will have a triennial review every three years to provide current assessment information to help determine the child's continued placement in special education. At the triennial evaluation, updated information is provided through re-examining many of the areas tested in the initial evaluation. The results of this evaluation, which is usually conducted by school officials, must be discussed at an IEP committee meeting.

Declassification Procedures of a Child in Special Education

The IEP committee is responsible for declassifying students previously classified with a disability who no longer meet the requirements for special education. The rationale for declassification is as follows:

- The child demonstrates effective compensatory skills.
- The student no longer exhibits difficulty in the classroom (no classroom impact on performance), despite a process deficit and discrepancy.
- The student no longer exhibits difficulty in the classroom (performance) or a discrepancy between ability and achievement (no classroom impact), despite a process deficit.

- The student no longer exhibits difficulty in the classroom (performance) or a process deficit (no classroom impact), despite a discrepancy between ability and achievement.
- Depending on state regulations, the child who is declassified may be entitled to transition services that offer up to one year of support following the declassification. However, testing modifications can continue after the student is declassified when the student graduates from high school or receives an IEP diploma (a diploma offered to children with disabilities who meet the criteria of their IEPs but do not meet district or state standards for graduation).

IEP Development

All students in special education are expected to leave school prepared to do the following:

- Live independently
- Enjoy self-determination
- Make choices
- Contribute to society
- Pursue meaningful careers
- Enjoy integration in the economic, political, social, cultural, and educational mainstream of American society

As previously discussed, the school district's committee on eligibility for special education services (IEP committee) is charged with ensuring that each student with a disability is educated to the maximum extent appropriate in classes and programs with their peers who do not have disabilities. For school-age students with disabilities, this committee must consider the supports, services, and program modifications necessary for a student to participate in general education classes and extracurricular and nonacademic activities. To encourage placement in the least restrictive environment, IDEA 2004 requires that all students in special education have an individualized education program (IEP).

The IEP is the key document developed by the parent and the child's teachers and related services personnel. It lays out how the child will receive a free appropriate public education in the least restrictive environment. Among other components, the IEP describes the child's academic achievement and functional performance, describes how the child will be included in the general education curriculum, establishes annual goals for the child and describes how those goals will be measured, states what special education and related services are needed by the child, describes how the child will be appropriately assessed including through the use of alternate assessments, and determines what accommodations may be appropriate for the child's instruction and assessments.

Components to Be Included in the IEP

According to IDEA 2004, the components of an IEP must include the following:

- A statement of the child's present levels of academic achievement and functional performance that includes the following information:
  - How the child's disability affects the child's involvement and progress in the general education curriculum
  - For preschool children, as appropriate, how the disability affects the child's participation in appropriate activities
  - For children with disabilities who take alternate assessments aligned to alternative achievement standards, a description of benchmarks or short-term objectives
- A statement of measurable annual goals, including academic and functional goals, designed to do the following:
  - Meet the child's needs that result from the disability to enable the child to be involved in and make progress in the general education curriculum.
  - Meet each of the child's other educational needs that result from the disability.
- A description of how the child's progress toward meeting the annual goals described above will be measured and when periodic reports on the child's progress toward the annual goals (such as quarterly or other periodic reports, issued concurrently with report cards) will be provided
- A statement of the special education and related services and supplementary aids and services, based on peer-reviewed research to the extent practicable, to be provided to the child, or on behalf of the child, and a statement of the program modifications or supports for school personnel that will be provided for the child

Questions and Answers About the IEP Under IDEA 2004

What is the time line for getting a child evaluated for a disability?

For a child to be eligible for special education and related services, the child must first be determined to have a disability. Parents, teachers, or other school officials who suspect that the child may have a disability would request that the child be evaluated by a multidisciplinary team to determine if the child has a disability and needs special education or related services as a result of the disability. Generally speaking, IDEA requires that a child be evaluated within 60 days once the parent has given consent for the evaluation. However, states may establish shorter or longer time frames in their own legislation or regulations, and those state-developed time lines would be binding.

Exceptions to the time line exist if the child moves from one district or state to another district or state after the evaluation was requested or if the parent refuses to make the child available for the evaluation. Under those circumstances, districts are required to make sufficient progress to ensure that a timely evaluation is conducted.

If a child moves from one district to another within the state, does the IEP follow the child?

No. The new local educational agency (LEA) is required to continue to provide a free appropriate public education to the child with a disability, including by providing services that are comparable to those services outlined in the child's original IEP. The new LEA is not required to implement the pre-existing IEP but may choose to do so at its own discretion. If the new LEA does not implement that IEP, the new LEA must work with the parent through the IEP team process to develop an IEP that is consistent with federal and state law.

If a child moves from one state to another, does the IEP follow the child?

No. The new LEA in the new state is required to provide a free appropriate public education to the child with a disability, including by providing services that are comparable to those services outlined in the child's original IEP. The LEA in the new state is not required to implement the pre-existing IEP but may choose to do so at its own discretion. If the new LEA does not implement that IEP, the new LEA in the new state must work with the parent through the IEP team process to develop an IEP that is consistent with federal and state law.

Additionally, because definitions of disability and eligibility vary from state to state, the LEA in the new state may require the child to be evaluated to determine whether the child is eligible to be identified as a child with a disability under that state's law. If the child is eligible for services under IDEA in the new state, an IEP must be developed and implemented for the child.

What if a parent doesn't provide
consent for evaluation or for services?

If a parent does not provide consent for an evaluation, the LEA has the authority to use the due process procedures to seek an order from a hearing officer requiring an evaluation. LEAs should use this authority sparingly.

If a parent does not provide consent for the provision of services, no special education or related services may be provided. The right of a parent to decide what educational services the child receives cannot be overturned using IDEA's due process procedures. If a parent indicates refusal both of consent for evaluations and consent for services, nothing in IDEA requires that an LEA use the due process procedures to proceed through the evaluation phase.

What methods are LEAs allowed to use to identify
a child as having a specific learning disability?

Almost half of the students identified as being disabled under IDEA are placed in the category of "specific learning disability" (SLD). To eliminate outdated methods of determining whether a child actually has an SLD and to respond to the need to identify children before they start to fail academically because of their disability, IDEA allows local districts significant new flexibility in developing appropriate methods of determining whether a child has an SLD.

However, IDEA does prohibit states from requiring that LEAs routinely use an IQ test as a part of the determination of specific learning disabilities. This means that the IQ-achievement discrepancy model, in which a specific learning disability is identified when there is a discrepancy between achievement and intellectual ability, cannot be mandated. States and LEAs are encouraged to look to research-based practices, especially models using response-to-intervention strategies, to determine whether a child has a specific learning disability. The Department of Education will develop guidance and provide technical assistance to states and LEAs using effective, scientifically based research to develop effective models of identification practices.

Must all children with disabilities
participate in state assessments?

Yes. Under the No Child Left Behind Act (NCLB), for the first time ever, states and local schools are held accountable for ensuring that all children—including children with disabilities—are learning. Children with disabilities must be included in the assessment system required under the No Child Left Behind Act, and schools must report their results through NCLB's adequate yearly progress structure. IDEA requires that the IEP team determine how the child with a disability is assessed, not whether the child is assessed. IDEA recognizes that children learn in different ways with different methods of instruction and assessment. The IEP team is required to determine which accommodations are necessary, how to instruct the child, and how to assess the child.

The IEP team can have a child with a disability take the regular state assessment; the regular state assessment with appropriate accommodations such as Braille, additional time, or having the instructions read to the child multiple times; an alternate assessment aligned to grade-level standards; or an alternate assessment aligned to alternate achievement standards. This array of assessment opportunities ensures that all students with disabilities can be assessed appropriately for individual and systemic accountability efforts.

Should all states have alternate assessments?

Yes. IDEA builds on the education reforms of the past decade by allowing states to develop appropriate alternate assessments aligned to grade-level standards for students with disabilities so that they can demonstrate what they know. Since 1997, IDEA has required that all states have alternate assessments. In 2004, IDEA was updated to allow states to develop alternate assessments tied to alternate achievement standards to allow for maximum flexibility in appropriately assessing students with disabilities. However, all decisions about which assessment a child with a disability should take are to be made by the IEP team.

Is there a conflict between IDEA and NCLB on assessments for students with disabilities?

No. IDEA and NCLB work in concert to ensure that students with disabilities are included in assessments and accountability systems. While IDEA focuses on the needs of the individual child, NCLB focuses on ensuring improved academic achievement for all students.

Is the IEP required to include benchmarks and short-term objectives for all students with disabilities?

No. IDEA was updated to align carefully with NCLB, ensuring that parents of students with disabilities get access to the same level of information about their children's academic performance as parents of all students without disabilities. For most students with disabilities, the IEP team includes a statement of the child's current performance, establishes annual goals, describes how those goals will be measured, and establishes a reporting cycle similar to that of all other students.

However, for those students with disabilities taking an alternate assessment aligned to alternate achievement standards, the IEP team is required to include benchmarks and short-term objectives. Since these students will typically not perform at or near grade level, measuring their progress requires a different approach, and using benchmarks and short-term objectives accommodate this need.

Who has to be part of the IEP team?

The IEP team is responsible for developing the IEP and ensuring its effective implementation so that the child with a disability can receive special education and related services. The IEP team must include the parents of the child with a disability, a regular education teacher (if the child is participating in the regular education environment), a special education teacher, and a representative of the school district. In addition, the parent and the school district can agree to add other members knowledgeable about related services or who have expertise about the child.

Do IEP team members need to be at every meeting?

To hold efficient and effective IEP team meetings, the parent and the LEA may agree to excuse any member of the IEP team from the meeting if that person's area of curriculum or related services is not being addressed.

The parent and the LEA may also agree to excuse any member of the IEP team from the meeting if their area of curriculum or related services is being addressed, but the team member will be required to submit input in writing to the parent and the LEA prior to the meeting.

The parent must provide written consent to the excusal of any IEP team member.

Can the IEP be amended without reconvening the whole IEP team?

Yes. To provide greater flexibility for parents and schools, IDEA allows the parent and the LEA to agree to amend or modify the IEP without reconvening the whole IEP team. Such an amendment or modification must be in writing to lay out clearly what has been modified or amended.

*Can IEP teams use modern technology to
develop the IEP and conduct meetings?*

Yes. To facilitate the meeting process, reduce paperwork, and make meetings more efficient, IDEA allows IEP teams to use computers to develop an IEP for a child with a disability instead of using typewriters or handwritten documents. Additionally, to accommodate busy work schedules for parents and school personnel, IDEA allows the parents to agree to use conference calls, video conferencing, or other alternative means of participation to conduct IEP meetings and other meetings required under IDEA, including resolution session meetings.

Conclusion

The IEP committee packet is a crucial piece of the special education process, because it represents the culmination of gathering information, evaluations, observations, intakes, professional opinions, and recommendations necessary for the proper educational direction of a child with a suspected disability. This information will be viewed by all the members of the IEP committee along with the parents and other individuals so designated, such as an advocate or lawyer. This packet is crucial because most of the IEP committee members will not be familiar with the child, and they will use the information gathered and forwarded to determine the child's educational future. Therefore, it is imperative that the MDT present the most thorough and practical information to the IEP committee.

Unless the student's IEP requires some other arrangement, the student with a disability must be educated in the school the child would have attended if he or she did not have a disability. The determination of the recommended placement is the final step in developing an IEP. The placement decision must address the full range of the student's cognitive, social, physical, linguistic, and communication needs. According to the LRE requirements of federal and state law and regulations, a student may be removed from the general education environment only when the nature or severity of the disability is such that the student's education cannot be satisfactorily achieved, even with the use of supplementary supports and services, in the general education setting.

If a child is classified with a disability, several other procedures will occur in the special education process. Some of these may occur during the year, at the end of the year, or every three years. These procedures are also part of due process rights for students with disabilities and their parents. The IEP committee handles many types of issues, but the three more common ones are special meetings, annual reviews, and triennial reviews. All of these meetings are for the sole purpose of protecting the rights of both the children and the parents. In the end, the IEP committee plays a very significant role within the school district. An effective IEP committee, working as an interdisciplinary team, can make a tremendous difference in the lives of children with disabilities. It is truly the link between the child and the child's educational future.

9

Transition Services for Students With Learning Disabilities

The Transitional Process

The last two decades have witnessed significant changes for people with disabilities, in large part due to the disability rights movement that, in many ways, paralleled the civil rights movement. While people with disabilities used to be thought of as an invisible minority, they now are a presence in all the media, commercial advertising, and many forms of public life. Changes in the laws and progress and technology have helped make these advances possible. Despite these gains, the barriers to acceptance remain: society's myths, fears, and stereotypes. Consequently, the efforts for change are ongoing. The implementation of transition services is a significant component of this pathway to acceptance.

Since the number of students with learning disabilities composes the largest number of individuals in the disability community (50.5 percent; Gargiulo, 2004), special education that assists the transition to adult life is a major concern for this population. The need for such services becomes more apparent as students with learning disabilities prepare for the adult world. Feelings of anxiety may arise because these students are uncertain about their futures, which may include postsecondary education, employment, and independent community living (Pierangelo & Giuliani, 2004). The legislation governing transition services was passed to prevent children with disabilities from being ill-prepared for postsecondary life. Since many aspects of learning disabilities continue throughout adulthood, it is imperative that students with learning disabilities be provided with a suitable transition plan to increase their chances of being productive members of society.

As many adults know from their own experience, adolescence is often the most difficult and unsettling period of adjustment in one's development. It is a time filled with physical, emotional, and social upheavals. Until a child leaves secondary school, parents and teachers may experience a sense of protective control over the child's life. This protective guidance normally involves educational, medical, financial, and social input to assist the child's growth. When the child leaves this setting, parents and other adults normally feel a personal struggle in letting go. A certain amount of apprehension associated with the child's entrance into the adult world is normal.

However, for the child with a learning disability, this developmental period can be fraught with even greater apprehension for a variety of reasons. Depending on the nature and severity of the learning disability, parents may play more of an ongoing role in their child's life even after the child leaves secondary education. Historically, parents and their children have spent years actively involved in IEP development and meetings, transitional IEP development, and eligibility committee meetings concerning educational and developmental welfare. Depending on the severity of the learning disability and its interference in making reasoned decisions, some parents may have to continue to make vital decisions affecting all aspects of their child's life.

Because planning for the future of a student with learning disabilities can arouse fear of the unknown, parents may tend to delay addressing these issues and instead focus only on the present. However, working through these fears and thinking about the child's best future interest has a greater chance of ensuring a meaningful outcome than avoidance or denial. Regardless of the nature and severity of the learning disability, educators and parents will be exposed to a transitional process during the child's school years that will provide a foundation for the adult world. This transitional process will include many facets of planning for the future and should be fully understood by everyone concerned each step of the way. Planning for the future is an investment in a child's well-being.

The Intent of Transition Services

For many years, educators have been concerned about the lack of success in adult life for students with disabilities. Many did not pursue further training and often did not receive postschool support and services. As these children "aged out" (became ineligible for a free and appropriate education, including the services and support of the educational system), their families felt that they were being dropped into a void. Although many services were available in the community, parents were left to their own devices, only finding out about such services and supports by chance. Parents and students were confronted with a complex array of service options and resources, each with unique roles, features, funding sources, forms, and eligibility requirements. A need for a collaborative, readily accessible system was obvious.

What seemed to be missing was the bridge between a student's school system and services for postschool life. As a result, the concept of transitional services was developed to bridge this gap and provide students with special needs a more structured path to adulthood.

The Importance of Transition Services for Individuals With Learning Disabilities

Even though transition planning has been mandated for all students with disabilities for more than ten years, transition planning for individuals with LD has lagged behind that for other groups. A major reason for this lack of attention has been an assumption that individuals with LD have a mild disability that primarily affects academic achievement; therefore, they must have the ability to move from secondary to postsecondary environments without a lot of difficulty. Unfortunately, this is not the case for many students with learning disabilities. The results of a number of recent studies suggest that many adolescents with LD do encounter difficulties in making the transition to adult life, including problems related to unemployment, underemployment, job changes, participation in community and leisure activities, pay, dependency on parents and others, satisfaction with employment, postsecondary academics, and functional skills.

The Introduction of Transition Services

In 1990, the laws governing the education of children with disabilities took a major step forward with the introduction of transition services.

The rules and regulations for the IDEA released in 1990 define transition services as

> A—a coordinated set of activities for a student, designed within an outcome-oriented process that promotes movement from school to postschool activities, including postsecondary education, vocational training, integrated employment (including supported employment), continuing and adult education, adult services, independent living, or community participation.

> B—the coordinated set of activities must be based on the individual student's needs, taking into account the student's preferences and interests; include instruction, community experience, the development of employment and other postschool adult living objectives and if appropriate, acquisition of daily living skills and functional evaluation. (34 C.F.R. § 300.18)

Simply put, *transition* is helping students and their families think about life after high school, identify long-range goals, and design the high school experience to ensure that students gain the skills and connections, the funds, and services in local school districts to assist in the transition process.

In May 1994, President Clinton signed the School to Work Opportunities Act. This act contains the blueprint to empower all individuals, including those with disabilities, to acquire the skills and experiences they need to procure gainful employment. This landmark bill demonstrates that transition is clearly now a national priority, important to ensure our economic viability as well as to offer every young person a chance at a productive life.

Every state receives federal special education moneys through Part B of IDEA, and in turn, most of these funds flow through to local school districts and other state-supported programs providing special education services. As a requirement of receiving these funds, programs are monitored by state education agencies.

The Individualized Transition Plan (ITP)

The IEP, as it has been defined over the years by legislation and court rulings, is not changed by the presence of the transition services section. The IEP is still a contract among the students, the parents, and the school. It is not a performance contract. The IEP spells out what the school will do (services and activities). If a service activity is written on the IEP, the school is responsible for performing it.

The IEP should contain information about transition services that the school district can only provide, directly or indirectly (by arranging for another agency to provide services coordinated with the school services). As in previous interpretations of the IEP, parents cannot be listed as responsible for achieving an outcome or providing a service. This is the school district's responsibility.

The individualized transition plan (ITP), though just one part of the overall IEP, is a very important piece of determining a child's future. The ITP should include long-term adult outcomes from which annual goals and objectives are defined.

The ITP should address the following:

- A statement of transition services should be responsive to the child's preferences, interests, and needs. The beginning date for the service should be provided.
- Annual goals and objectives, such as employment services and living arrangements, should be described.
- Long-term adult outcomes should include statements regarding the child's performance in employment, postsecondary education, and community living.
- A coordinated set of activities must be included in the ITP. This set must demonstrate the use of various strategies, including community experiences, adult living objectives, and instruction. If one of these activities is not included in a particular year, then the ITP must explain why that activity is not reflected in any part of the student's program. Activities of daily living and functional vocational evaluation activities also should be included.
- The participants involved in the planning and development of the ITP should be listed.

Transition Services

Transition services are aimed at providing students and their families with the practical and experiential skills and knowledge that will assist in a successful transition to adult life. The services included in the transition process may involve both students and parents. Although transition services are provided in each of the following areas, it is important to understand that not every student with disabilities needs to receive all of these services:

- Employment services
- Living arrangements
- Leisure/recreational services
- Transportation services
- Financial services
- Postsecondary education services
- Assistive technology
- Medical services

As an educator working with students with learning disabilities, it is crucial for you to become familiar with the aspects of transition that will impact on this specific population so that you can assist both parents and the student in the process of moving toward adulthood. A brief explanation of the areas involved in the transition process follows.

Special Considerations for Students With Learning Disabilities

Several special factors need to be considered in transition planning for students with LD. One of these factors is the dropout rate. Students with LD are at great risk for dropping out of school. Recent dropout estimates for this population range from 17 to 42 percent (Scanlon & Mellard, 2002). Dropping out engenders numerous consequences relating to job opportunities, income, and self-esteem. Among students with LD, those most at risk for dropping out are boys from urban communities and low-income homes who are racial minorities. Such students should receive intensified support, and their progress should be monitored.

According to the Council for Learning Disabilities (2004), another critical factor in transition planning for students with LD is individualized planning that matches a student's post–high school goals. Because the population of students with disabilities is so heterogeneous, a wide range of postsecondary goals and transition planning should be considered. For some students, the next step after high school will be employment, for other students it will be further career or technical training, and for still others it will be attending a four-year college or university. To be successful in the post–high school environment, these students must be provided with appropriate training and experiences. For example, for a student whose postsecondary goal is attending a university, the high school curriculum must include participation in college preparatory courses and the development of independent study skills. For a student whose postsecondary goal is employment, the high school curriculum must include participation in career/technical education courses and work experiences. For all students, the curriculum should include the development of self-determination skills, social and inter-personal skills, community integration and participation skills, and independent living skills, if appropriate.

A final critical aspect of transition planning for students with LD is self-determination, which has been defined as "one's ability to define and achieve goals based on a foundation of knowing and valuing oneself" (Field & Hoffman, 1994, p. 164). Self-determination is highly related to positive adult outcomes. For example, Wehmeyer and Schwartz (1997) found that students with high levels of self-determination were more likely to be employed for pay, have a savings or checking account, and have expressed an interest in living outside of the home. Skills related to self-determination include self-evaluation, self-awareness, self-knowledge, self-management, choice making, decision making, problem solving, goal setting and attainment, and social collaboration (Field, Hoffman, & Spezia, 1998).

Employment Services

Crossing the threshold from the world of school to the world of work brings a significant change in everyone's life. School is an entitle-ment, meaning that it is an environment that our system of government supplies for all our citizens. The workplace is the opposite; no one is "entitled" to a job. The workplace is governed by the competitive mar-ket, and students with or without disabilities have to be able to function in that setting, or they will not survive.

One of the first and most important aspects of transition planning is the preparation of some students for the world of work. This very prac-tical issue can raise many concerns. However, with the proper informa-tion and resources, this phase of the transition process can also be rewarding. Parents and teachers must fully understand the available options to help the child make the best decision for the child's future. The first step in planning for employment may begin with vocational assessments to help determine the best direction based on the child's interests and skill levels.

Vocational Assessments

One of the techniques used to determine a child's interests, apti-tudes, and skills is a vocational assessment. A vocational assessment is the responsibility of the district's special education program. It begins by assessing referrals for special education services and continues throughout subsequent annual reviews. The planning of transitional services includes the eligibility committee's development of transitional employment goals and objectives based on the child's needs, prefer-ences, and interests. These will be identified through the child-centered vocational assessment process.

A good vocational assessment should include the collection and analysis of information about a child's vocational aptitudes, skills, expressed interests, and occupational exploration history (e.g., volun-teer experiences, part-time or summer employment, club activities). The collection of this information should also take into account the child's language, culture, and family.

A Level I vocational assessment is administered at the beginning of a child's transitional process, usually around age 13 or 14, and is based on the student's abilities, expressed interests, and needs. The Level I assessment may include the review of existing school information and the conduct of informal interviews. A trained vocational evaluator or knowledgeable special education teacher should be designated to collect Level I assessment data. The information gathered for analyses should include existing information from the following sources:

- Cumulative records
- Student interviews
- Parent/guardian and teacher interviews
- Special education eligibility data
- A review of the child's aptitudes
- Achievements
- Interests
- Behaviors
- Occupational exploration activities

The informal student interview involved in a Level I assessment should consider the student's vocational interests, interpersonal rela-tionship skills, and adaptive behavior.

A Level II vocational assessment usually includes the administration of one or more formal vocational evaluations. A Level II assessment fol-lows and is based on the analyses obtained from the Level I assessment. It may be recommended by the eligibility committee at any time to determine the level of a student's vocational skills, aptitudes, and inter-ests but not before the age of 12. The same knowledgeable staff members involved in prior assessments should be used. Collected data should include the following:

- Writing
- Learning styles
- Interest inventory

- Motor skills (dexterity, speed, tool use, strength, coordination)
- Spatial discrimination
- Verbal reading
- Perception (visual/auditory/tactile)
- Speaking numerical (measurement, money skills)
- Comprehension (task learning, problem solving)
- Attention (staying on-task)

A Level III vocational assessment is a comprehensive vocational evaluation that focuses on real or simulated work experiences. This assessment is the basis for vocational counseling. Unlike Level I and Level II assessments, a trained vocational evaluator should administer or supervise this level of assessment. Level III assessment options include the following:

- *Vocational evaluations:* These compare the student's aptitudes and interests to job performance to predict vocational success in specific areas. Work samples must be valid and reliable.
- *Situational vocational assessments that occur in real work settings:* This on-the-job assessment considers what has been learned and how.
- *Work-study assessments:* These are progress reports from supervisors or mentors that provide information on the student's job performance. A standard observational checklist may be utilized.

Postsecondary Educational Services

If students plan a postsecondary educational program, they may benefit from two types of assessments:

- *General assessments of postsecondary education skills* are necessary to determine academic skills, critical thinking skills, requirements for reasonable accommodations, social behaviors, interpersonal skills, self-advocacy and self-determination skills, learning strategies, and time management or organizational skills. This information is usually obtained through consultation with peers, teachers, or a self-evaluation.
- *Assessments specific to field of study or setting* are necessary to assess needs in relation to daily living skills that may be experienced in a classroom setting or college campus, such as dormitory living versus commuting, lab work, large lecture versus seminar courses.

Parents should be encouraged to visit campuses that provide supportive services for children with disabilities. Sources of information regarding colleges that provide these services can be obtained in the local libraries, bookstores, or high school guidance offices.

Leisure/Recreational Experiences

Leisure is an activity that we do by choice for relaxation rather than for money as part of our job. When a student with a learning disability is involved in the transition from school to adult life, a healthy part of this journey should include leisure activities. Teachers and parents may generally discover the student's leisure interests by having the child sample a variety of activities and learning which ones are the most interesting and exciting. Parents of very young children in today's society normally expose them to a wide variety of experiences, such as the following:

- Dance classes
- Sports activities
- Little League
- Cultural experiences
- Music lessons
- Travel
- Scouting
- Art lessons

As students without disabilities grow older, this process of sampling leisure interests depends less on their parents and more on their peer group. For young people with learning disabilities, however, teachers, parents, and other family members may continue to guide or structure leisure experiences. This extended period of guidance and involvement should be considered a realistic part of a student's transitional process to adulthood. Learning specific leisure skills can be an important component for successful integration into community recreation programs. Research has shown that leisure skill training contributes to a sense of competence, social interaction, and appropriate behavior.

Advantages of Special Leisure Programs

One of the conflicts that teachers and parents must address is whether the child should participate in activities designed specifically for people with disabilities or enter activities that are geared for a more mainstream population. The advantages of a special program designed for children with disabilities are the following:

- They may allow the only opportunity for some children with severe disabilities to participate (e.g., Special Olympics).

- They allow for a sense of group identity.
- They provide a setting for social interaction.
- They create a more level playing field so that the individual's abilities become the focus rather than the disability.

On the other hand, concentrating on disabled-only activities may unnecessarily exclude individuals from many leisure opportunities and prevent interaction with the nondisabled community.

Individual Concerns When Faced With Leisure Activities

One of the greatest concerns of individuals with disabilities is the problems they may face assimilating into the social world. Many students receive special services while in school that expose them to other children with disabilities. This social interaction and connection provide a foundation for improving social skills. However, once the school experience ends and the individual with a disability is confronted with the mainstream world, many of these social opportunities are not available, and social isolation is often the result. Social isolation can be a painful aspect of entering adulthood for individuals with learning disabilities. Therefore, parents play a crucial role in assisting their children by providing exposure to leisure and recreational activities. Parents may often find themselves as the only agent for this particular aspect of life, especially once the child leaves the school setting.

Parents and professionals should be aware of the enormous benefit of recreational activities in building social and personal confidence. Having a learning disability should not preclude a person from activities that enhance enjoyment. It is always important in one's life to maintain a balance between work and play.

Recreation activities have been one of the most visible areas of change for people with learning disabilities. There is hardly a sport activity that cannot include the participation of people with learning disabilities. For those who accept the challenge, nothing is off-limits. Not everyone needs or wants to be a superstar. But everyone can attain a level of confidence in an interesting activity. Parents and educators need to be supportive and encouraging to help their children develop those interests and skills, because for all people, the mastery of tasks increases self-esteem.

Postsecondary Education Options

Some students with disabilities may be capable of graduating high school with all the requirements for college and moving on to a postsecondary education experience. A number of years ago, students with disabilities had limited choices when it came to choosing a college or university that could provide accommodations. With the advent of the Americans with Disabilities Act (ADA) and the disabilities rights movement, however, accommodations for students with disabilities have become relatively commonplace. However, many colleges may require documentation of the presence of a learning disability. According to Barr, Hartman, and Spillane (2005), documentation is defined in the following manner:

> A high school student with a learning disability is one who has been evaluated by professionals. Such professionals (a school psychologist or educational diagnostician), after reviewing the results of various tests and other evidence, provide for each student a written diagnosis that a learning disability exists. Recommendations for accommodative services and programs are also usually part of the written document. This document can serve as a vehicle for the student to understand his or her strengths and weaknesses, as well as a "ticket" to obtain the accommodative services necessary to participate in regular college programs. There are several points for a student planning to go to college to keep in mind concerning the documentation of a learning disability: IDEA requires re-evaluations to be conducted at least every three years; therefore, students with learning disabilities may be wise to have a comprehensive re-evaluation conducted close to high school graduation time. This will ensure, for students who are going directly into postsecondary education, that the documentation that they take with them will be timely. If the student is unable to be evaluated close to graduation from high school, it is possible that a college or university, after receiving documentation, may decide that the documentation is too old. This may occur if the college or university feels that the information does not adequately describe the student's current academic strengths and weaknesses, learning styles, etc. Such current information can be invaluable in determining the most appropriate accommodations for the student. While an agreed upon definition does not exist within the postsecondary/disability community of "how old is too old," evidence from the field suggests a range of two-five years. While it is ultimately the student's responsibility to obtain necessary documentation, some colleges and universities do provide testing services. Students should ask about campus-based possibilities before going to a private diagnostician. Students

and parents should study and discuss the documentation in order to fully understand what it conveys about the student's strengths, weaknesses, and recommended accommodative services. If the report is not clear, discuss it with the school psychologist or whoever has prepared it. Many high schools routinely destroy copies of student records after a predetermined number of years. As students with learning disabilities will need copies of select items in their records to show to the college or university as documentation of their disability, students should make sure that they have complete copies of all of their records upon leaving high school. (pp. 1–2)

When to Begin College Planning

IDEA requires that the IEP team consider postschool goals when the student is about to enter high school at about age 14. Beginning at age 16 (or younger, if appropriate), a statement of transition services the student will need must be included in the IEP. High school experiences, both academic and social, greatly influence future options for all students. For adolescents with disabilities, these experiences are especially pivotal.

Transition plans should be grounded in the student's goals and vision for life as an adult, career interests, extracurricular and community activities, and the skills the student needs to progress toward his goals. Planning should include preparation for proficiency tests and other assessments needed for postsecondary academic work (e.g., SATs), as well as the development of self-determination and self-advocacy skills.

During the last two years of high school, diagnostic testing should be conducted to further define the LD or ADHD. Colleges require documentation of a disability (i.e., results of tests indicating the presence of a disability) to provide support services; having an IEP or Section 504 plan in high school is not enough documentation to obtain services from colleges. Students entering postsecondary programs need to present current assessment data to receive accommodations.

Even for students who have struggled academically in high school, postsecondary education may very well be a possibility. Students who wonder whether college is a realistic option can explore summer precollege courses for high school students who have completed their junior or senior year. Alternatively, students can take a college course the summer before they enroll to get to know the campus, learn how to use the library, and sharpen their study strategies and time management skills.

Colleges offer an opportunity for individuals with disabilities to continue their educations and earn tangible evidence of education, such as a certificate or degree. Junior and community colleges offer a variety of courses that, upon their successful completion, may lead to a certificate or associate's degree. Community colleges are publicly funded, have either no or low-cost tuition, and offer a wide range of programs, including vocational and occupational courses. They exist in or near many communities; generally the only admissions requirement is a high school diploma or its equivalent. Junior colleges are usually privately supported, and most provide programs in the liberal arts field. Four-year colleges and universities offer programs of study that lead to a bachelor's degree after successful completion of four years of prescribed course work.

Understanding Legal Rights Pertaining to Postsecondary Education

Once students with disabilities graduate from high school, they are no longer eligible for services provided by the school system and will not have an IEP. If they have been receiving rehabilitation services as part of their transition plans, however, they can continue to receive them. They will also have an individual written rehabilitation plan (IWRP) and may be eligible for services such as postsecondary education, counseling, and vocational evaluation and assessment.

ADA bars discrimination against students with disabilities in the college application process. Once admitted, students may request reasonable accommodations to allow them to participate in courses, exams, and other activities. Most colleges and universities have a disability support services office to assist in providing accommodations.

Identifying the Desirable Characteristics of a College

Once the student's strengths, learning needs, and level of support needed have been delineated, it is time to look at the characteristics of colleges that might be a good match for the student. Consider various types of colleges: two-year colleges, public community colleges, private junior colleges, four-year colleges and universities, as well as, eventually, graduate and professional schools. Students with LD can succeed in all types of schools, including the most prestigious.

Students must determine the characteristics of colleges that will make them happy and support their success. For example, how big is their high school? Will they feel more comfortable in a larger or a smaller college? Will they be happier in an urban or a rural area? Can they meet the academic requirements? Should they find a college that doesn't impose rigid prerequisites? Should they consider enrolling part-time rather than taking a full course load? What are their academic and extracurricular interests?

In looking at colleges, students may also want to consider whether progressive attitudes toward instruction prevail. Colleges that are using instructional techniques and electronic technology in a flexible way can increase students' success. For example, if courses are Web based so lecture notes or videos of presentations are available online and can be viewed multiple times, then students have natural supports built into a course.

Nevertheless, according to the Heath Resource Center (Henderson, 2001), a student can get a good idea about the nature of the college by asking questions such as the following:

- Does this college require standardized college admissions test scores? If so, what is the range of scores for those admitted?
- For how many students with learning disabilities does the campus currently provide services?
- What major fields of study are offered?
- What types of academic accommodations does this campus typically provide to students with learning disabilities?
- Will this college provide the specific accommodations that I need?
- What documentation of a learning disability is necessary to arrange academic accommodations for admitted students?
- How is the confidentiality of applicants' records, as well as those of enrolled students, protected? Where does the college publish Family Education Rights and Privacy Act guidelines that I can review?
- How is information related to the documentation of a learning disability used? By whom?
- Does the college or university have someone available who is trained and understands the needs of adults with learning disabilities?
- What academic and personal characteristics have been found important for students with learning disabilities to succeed at this college?
- How many students with learning disabilities have graduated in the past five years?
- What is the tuition? Are there additional fees for services related to learning disabilities? If so, what services beyond those required by Section 504 and the ADA do you get for those fees?

In addition to talking with college staff, try to arrange a meeting with several college students with learning disabilities and talk with them about the services they receive and their experiences on campus. Such a meeting can be requested when scheduling the interview with the college staff. While you will certainly be interested in the answers to your specific questions, the impressions that you get during conversations with students will be equally important and may serve as a way to make final refinements to the short list.

Students with disabilities must also look at other factors. They should investigate the support services offered by candidate colleges, discuss them with college staff (e.g., personnel in the Office of Disability Support Services), and verify that the services advertised by the college will actually be available. For example, is tutoring available? Will extended time be allowed for taking tests? Is someone available to help with taking notes or preparing written work? Will college policies allow extended time to complete a course of study so that fewer classes may be taken over a longer time? Furthermore, students with LD must decide whether and to whom to disclose the presence of the disability. To obtain support services, students must self-disclose their disabilities to the school's office of disability support services. That office will notify professors of the necessary accommodations. Students are not required to give faculty information about a disability, but to obtain the best coursework accommodations, they must be able to explain their needs to instructors. Therefore, students will want to investigate specific classes before they register for them. Some strategies for becoming informed about classes are listed below:

- *Participate in orientation programs.* These programs provide opportunities to become familiar with campus life and to ask questions of continuing students and advisors about classes, faculty, resources, and services.
- *Don't procrastinate.* Do not wait until the last minute to begin gathering information about courses and professors. Most offices for disability support services will allow students with disabilities to register a few days before other students.
- *Talk to other students.* Other students are an excellent source of information about classes and professors.
- *Audit classes.* It is possible to observe a class for a limited time to determine whether it is right for you. Students who audit a course are not responsible for exams or assignments.
- *Check the Internet.* Most colleges and universities offer an increasing amount of information, including course syllabi (outlines of the courses), objectives, textbooks, readings, and assignments.
- *Meet the professor.* Professors have scheduled office hours to answer questions about the course. Getting the textbooks and

reading list ahead of time also allows students an opportunity to get a head start on the course.

For many individuals with LD, the transition to adulthood is a time of positive self-discovery, but the process does involve trial and error. Goals and successes can sometimes be elusive, and the hidden nature of LD can pose special challenges. Careful preparation for the transition to college can help.

Disability-Related Support Services

Many college campuses have an office of student services or special services for those with disabilities. Others have designated the dean of students or some other administrator to provide information and to coordinate necessary services and accommodations. At vocational schools or other training programs, the person responsible for disability services can usually provide needed information. Also, many publications have information about the policies and programs that individual colleges and universities have established to address the needs of students with disabilities.

Assistive Technology

Technology has become ubiquitous as a tool for teachers and students. The Technology-Related Assistance for Individuals with Disabilities Act of 1988 (Tech Act) was designed to enhance the availability and quality of assistive technology (AT) devices and services to all individuals and their families throughout the United States. IDEA uses the same definitions for assistive technology as the Tech Act and mandates that assistive technology be considered in developing IEPs for students with disabilities. IDEA also emphasizes access to the general education curriculum for all students with disabilities.

The Tech Act and IDEA define an AT device as any item, piece of equipment, or product system (whether acquired off the shelf, modified, or customized) that is used to increase, maintain, or improve the functional capabilities of a student with a disability. AT devices may be categorized as no technology, low technology, or high technology.

No-technology or *no-tech* refers to any assistive device that is not electronic. No-tech items range from a piece of foam glued onto the corners of book pages to make turning easier to a study carrel to reduce distraction. *Low-technology* or *low-tech* devices are electronic but do not include highly sophisticated computer components; these might be an electronic voice-recording device or a "talking watch" (Behrmann & Schaff, 2001). *High-technology* or *high-tech* devices utilize complex, multifunction technology and usually include a computer and associated software.

Lahm and Morrissette (1994) identified a number of areas of instruction in which AT can assist students. Six of these are described here: (1) organization, (2) note taking, (3) writing, (4) academic productivity, (5) access to reference and general educational materials, and (6) cognitive assistance.

Organization

Low-tech solutions include teaching students to organize their thoughts or work using flowcharting, task analysis, webbing, and outlining. These strategies can also be accomplished using high-tech, graphic, software-based organizers to assist students in developing and structuring ideas. Such graphic organizers allow students to manipulate and reconfigure brainstormed ideas and color code and group those ideas in ways that visually represent their thoughts. Another high-tech solution might be the outline function of word processing software, which lets students set out major ideas or topics and then add subcategories of information. Using the Internet, local area networks, or LCD projection systems enables students and their teachers to collaborate, give feedback, and modify these applications either as a group or individually at different times.

Note Taking

A simple, no-tech approach to note taking is for the teacher to provide copies of structured outlines in which students fill in information. Mid- and high-tech methods include the following:

- Videotaping class sessions for visual learners or those who are unable to attend class for extended periods
- Sending webcam photography across the Internet to allow students to see and hear what is happening in class (for students who are unable to attend class)
- Sending class notes or presentations to students via e-mail
- Translating print-based notes to voice by using optical character recognition (OCR) software with a voice synthesizer
- Using notebook computers, personal digital assistants (PDAs), or portable word processing keyboards to help students with the mechanics of note taking

Writing

Computers may be the most important application of assistive technology for students with mild disabilities. Writing barriers for students with mild disabilities include the following:

- *Mechanics:* Spelling, grammar, and punctuation errors
- *Process:* Generating ideas, organizing, drafting, editing, revising, and producing a neat, clear final copy
- *Motivation:* Interest in writing

Grammar- and spell-checkers, dictionaries, and thesaurus programs assist with the mechanics of writing. Macros can insert an entire phrase with the touch of a single key. Word prediction features help students recall or spell words.

During the writing process, computers can allow teachers to make suggestions on the student's draft. If computers are networked, students can read each other's work and make recommendations for revision. Computer editing also reduces or eliminates problems such as multiple erasures, torn papers, and poor handwriting. The final copy is neat and legible.

Motivation is often increased through the desktop publishing and multimedia capabilities of computers. A variety of fonts and styles allow students to customize their writing and highlight important features. Graphic images, drawings, video, and audio can provide interest or highlight ideas. Multimedia gives the student the means and the motivation to generate new and more complex ideas. For early writers, some programs allow students to write with pictures or symbols as well as text. For example, the student may be able to select a series of pictures to represent an idea, then see the pictures transformed into words, hear them read by a synthesizer, and edit them.

Academic Productivity

Tools that assist productivity can be hardware based, software based, or both. Calculators, for example, can be separate, multifunction devices or part of a computer's software. Spreadsheets, databases, and graphics software enhance productivity in calculating, categorizing, grouping, and predicting events. The Internet, computers, and PDAs can also aid productivity in note taking, obtaining assignments, accessing reference material and help from experts, and communicating with peers. Instead of relying on the telephone, students are increasingly sharing documents across networks and as e-mail attachments and using instant messaging.

Access to Reference and General Educational Materials

Access to the general education curriculum is emphasized by IDEA. This includes the ability to obtain materials as well as the ability to understand and use them. Many students with mild disabilities have difficulty gathering and synthesizing information for their academic work. In this arena, Internet communications, multimedia, and universal design are providing new learning tools.

Internet communications can transport students beyond their physical environments, allowing them to interact with people far away and engage in interactive learning experiences. This is particularly appropriate for individuals who are easily distracted when going to new and busy environments, such as the library; who are poorly motivated; or who have difficulty with reading or writing. Students can establish "compupals" via e-mail or instant messaging with other students, which often motivates them to generate more text and thus gain more experience in writing. Students can also access electronic multimedia encyclopedias, library references, and online publications. However, these experiences should be structured, because it is easy to get distracted or lost as opportunities are explored.

Multimedia tools are another way in which information can be made accessible to students. Multimedia use of text, speech, graphics, pictures, audio, and video in reference-based software is especially effective in meeting the heterogeneous learning needs of students with mild disabilities. While a picture can be worth a thousand words to one student, audio- or text-based descriptive video or graphic supports may help another student focus on the most important features of the materials.

Used in conjunction with assistive technology, e-books can use the power of multimedia to motivate students to read. They include high-interest stories: The computer reads each page of the story aloud, highlighting the words as they are read. Fonts and colors can be changed to reduce distraction. Additional clicks of the mouse result in pronunciation of syllables and a definition of the word. When the student clicks on a picture, a label appears. A verbal pronunciation of the label is offered when the student clicks the mouse again. Word definitions can be added by electronic dictionaries and thesaurus. These books are available in multiple languages, including English and Spanish, so students can read in their native language while being exposed to a second language.

The Center for Applied Special Technology (CAST) promotes the concept of universal design (Rose & Meyer, 2000), which asserts that alternatives integrated into the general curriculum can provide access to all students, including those with a range of backgrounds, learning styles, or abilities. Providing material in digital form, which can easily be translated, modified, or presented in different ways, can often attain the goal of universal design.

Cognitive Assistance

A vast array of application program software is available for instructing students through tutorials, drill and practice, problem solving, and simulations. Many of the assistive technologies described previously can be combined with instructional programs to develop and improve cognitive, reading, and problem-solving skills. Prompting and scheduling through PDAs, pagers, and Internet software also can assist students in remembering assignments or important tasks. These devices can help students to follow directions or a sequence of events, establish to-do lists, take and retrieve notes, check spelling, or look up words in a dictionary.

Special educators are familiar with the need to create or customize instructional materials to meet the varied needs of students with learning disabilities. Today, assistive technology can be more specifically targeted to address an individual's needs through the emergent power and flexibility of electronic tools and the ways in which they are combined and used. These innovations affect teaching and learning as well as individual capabilities. For students with learning disabilities, assistive technology can help to balance weak areas of learning by leveraging strong areas.

Glossary

Accommodations—Techniques and materials that allow individuals with LD to complete school or work tasks with greater ease and effectiveness

Assistive technology—Equipment that enhances the ability of students and employees to be more efficient and successful. For individuals with LD, computer grammar checkers, an overhead projector used by a teacher, or the audiovisual information delivered through a CD-ROM would be typical examples.

Attention deficit disorder (ADD)—A severe difficulty in focusing and maintaining attention. Often leads to learning and behavior problems at home, school, and work. Also called attention deficit hyperactivity disorder (ADHD).

Brain imaging techniques—Noninvasive techniques for studying the activity of living brains. Includes brain electrical activity mapping (BEAM), computerized axial tomography (CAT), and magnetic resonance imaging (MRI).

Brain injury—The physical damage to brain tissue or structure that occurs before, during, or after birth that is verified by EEG, MRI, CAT, or a similar examination rather than by observation of performance. When caused by an accident, the damage may be called traumatic brain injury (TBI).

Collaboration—A program model in which the LD teacher demonstrates for or team-teaches with the general classroom teacher to help a student with LD be successful in a regular classroom

Developmental aphasia—A severe language disorder that is presumed to be due to brain injury rather than a developmental delay in the normal acquisition of language

Direct instruction—An instructional approach to academic subjects that emphasizes the use of carefully sequenced steps, including demonstration, modeling, guided practice, and independent application

Dyscalculia—A severe difficulty in understanding and using symbols or functions needed for success in mathematics

Dysgraphia—A severe difficulty in producing handwriting that is legible and written at an age-appropriate speed

Dyslexia—A severe difficulty in understanding or using one or more areas of language, including listening, speaking, reading, writing, and spelling

Dysnomia—A marked difficulty in remembering names or recalling words needed for oral or written language

Dyspraxia—A severe difficulty in performing drawing, writing, buttoning, and other tasks requiring fine motor skill or in sequencing the necessary movements

Learned helplessness—A tendency to be a passive learner who depends on others for decisions and guidance. In individuals with LD, continued struggle and failure can heighten this lack of self-confidence.

Learning modalities—Approaches to assessment or instruction stressing the auditory, visual, or tactile avenues for learning and customized to the individual

Learning strategy approaches—Instructional approaches that focus on efficient ways to learn rather than on curriculum. Include specific techniques for organizing, actively interacting with material, memorizing, and monitoring any content or subject.

Learning styles—Approaches to assessment or instruction emphasizing the variations in temperament, attitude, and preferred manner of tackling a task. Typically considered are styles along the active/passive, reflective/impulsive, or verbal/spatial dimensions.

Locus of control—The tendency to attribute success and difficulties either to internal factors, such as effort, or to external factors, such as chance. Individuals with learning disabilities tend to blame failure on themselves and achievement on luck, leading to frustration and passivity.

Metacognitive learning—Instructional approaches emphasizing awareness of the cognitive processes that facilitate one's own learning and its application to academic and work assignments. Typical metacognitive techniques include systematic rehearsal of steps or conscious selection among strategies for completing a task.

Minimal brain dysfunction (MBD)—A medical and psychological term originally used to refer to the learning difficulties that seemed to result from identified or presumed damage to the brain. Reflects a medical rather than an educational or vocational orientation.

Multisensory learning—An instructional approach that combines auditory, visual, and tactile elements into a learning task. Tracing sandpaper numbers while saying a number fact aloud would be a multisensory learning activity.

Neuropsychological examination—A series of tasks that allow observation of performance that is presumed to be related to the intactness of brain function

Perceptual handicap—Difficulty in accurately processing, organizing, and discriminating among visual, auditory, or tactile information. A person with a perceptual handicap may say that *cap* and *cup* sound the same or that *b* and *d* look the same. However, wearing glasses or hearing aids does not necessarily indicate a perceptual handicap.

Prereferral process—A procedure in which special and regular teachers develop trial strategies to help a student showing difficulty with learning remain in the regular classroom

Resource program—A program model in which a student with LD is in a regular classroom for most of each day but also receives regularly scheduled individual services in a specialized LD resource classroom

Self-advocacy—The development of specific skills and understandings that enable children and adults to explain their specific learning disabilities to others and cope positively with the attitudes of peers, parents, teachers, and employers

Specific language disability (SLD)—A severe difficulty in some aspect of listening, speaking, reading, writing, or spelling while skills in the other areas are age-appropriate. Also called specific language learning disability (SLLD).

Specific learning disability (SLD)—The official term used in federal legislation to refer to difficulty in certain areas of learning rather than in all areas of learning. Synonymous with *learning disabilities.*

Transition—Commonly used to refer to the change from secondary school to postsecondary programs, work, and independent living typical of young adults

References

Abel, E. (1985). Combining alcohol & marijuana increases miscarriage. *Teratology, 31,* 35–40.

Akron Children's Hospital. (2003). *Tips to grow by: Learning disabilities.* Retrieved September 10, 2005, from www.akronchildrens.org

Alexander, D., Gray, D. B., & Lyon, G. R. (1993). Conclusions and future directions. In G. R. Lyon, D. B. Gray, J. F. Kavanagh, & N. A. Krasnegor (Eds.), *Better understanding of learning disabilities: New views from research and their implications for education and public policies* (pp. 1–13). Baltimore: Paul Brooks.

American Psychiatric Association. (1994). *Diagnostic and statistical manual of mental disorders* (4th ed.). Washington, DC: Author.

Ashbaker, M. H., & Swanson, H. L. (1996). Short-term memory and working memory operations and their contributions to reading in adolescents with and without learning disabilities. *Journal of Abnormal Child Psychology, 18,* 29–45.

Barkley, R. A. (1990). *Attention deficit hyperactivity disorder: A handbook for diagnosis and treatment.* New York: Guilford.

Barkley, R. A. (1997). Behavioral inhibition, sustained attention, and executive functions: Constructing a unifying theory of ADHD. *Psychological Bulletin, 121*(1), 65–94.

Barr, V. M., Hartman, R. C., & Spillane, S. A. (2005). *Getting ready for college: Advising high school students with learning disabilities.* Washington, DC: HEATH Resource Center. Available from www.kidsource.com/heath/gr.html

Behrmann, M., & Schaff, J. (2001). Assisting educators with assistive technology: Enabling children to achieve independence in living and learning. *Children and Families 42*(3), 24–28.

Bell, S. M., McCallum, R. S., & Cox, E. A. (2003). Toward a research-based assessment of dyslexia: Using cognitive measures to identify reading disabilities. *Journal of Learning Disabilities, 36,* 505–515.

Bender, W. N. (2001). *Learning disabilities: Characteristics, identification, and teaching strategies* (4th ed.). Boston: Allyn & Bacon.

Bender, W. N. (2002). *Differentiating instruction for students with learning disabilities: Best practices for general and special educators.* Thousand Oaks, CA: Corwin Press.

Bishop, E. G., Cherny, S. S., Corley, R., Plomin, R., DeFries, J. C., & Hewitt, J. K. (2003). Developmental genetic analysis of general cognitive ability from 1 to 12 years in a sample of adoptees, biological siblings, and twins. *Intelligence, 31,* 31–49.

Bowe, F. (2005). *Making inclusion work.* Upper Saddle River, NJ: Pearson/Merrill-Prentice Hall.

Bradshaw, J. (2001). *Developmental disorders of the fronto-striatal system.* Philadelphia: Psychiatric Press.

Bryan, T. A. (1997). Assessing the personal and social status of students with learning disabilities. *Learning Disabilities Research & Practice, 12*(1), 63–76.

Bryan, T. A., Bay, M., Lopez-Reyna, N., & Donahue, M. (1991). Characteristics of students with learning disabilities: A summary of the extant data base and its implications for educational programs. In J. W. Lloyd, N. N. Singh, & A. C. Repp (Eds.), *The regular education initiative: Alternative perspectives* (pp. 121–131). Sycamore, IL: Thomson Brooks/Cole.

Bryan, T. A., & Sullivan-Burstein, K. (1998). Teacher-selected strategies for improving homework completion. *Remedial and Special Education, 19,* 263–273.

Centers for Disease Control and Prevention (CDC). (2001). *Women and smoking: A report of the Surgeon General.* Retrieved September 19, 2005, from www.surgeongeneral .gov/library/womenandtobacco/

Centers for Disease Control and Prevention (CDC). (2004). *About the childhood lead poisoning prevention program (CLPPP).* Retrieved September 10, 2005, from www.cdc .gov/nceh/lead/about/program.htm

Chandler, J. (2004). *Learning disorders, learning disabilities.* Retrieved September 10, 2005, from http://jamesdauntchandler.tripod.com/learning/learningpamphlet.htm

Ciocci, S. R. (2002). *Auditory processing disorders: An overview* (Eric Digest E364). Arlington, VA: ERIC Clearinghouse on Disabilities and Gifted Education, Council for Exceptional Children. (ERIC Document Reproduction Service No. ED474303)

Clements, S. D. (1966). Minimal brain dysfunction in children (NINDS Monograph No. 3, Public Health Service Bulletin No. 1415). Washington, DC: U.S. Department of Health, Education and Welfare.

Coles, C. D., Brown, R. T., Smith, I. E., Platzman, K. A., Erickson, S., & Falek, A. (1991). Effects of prenatal alcohol exposure at school age I: Physical and cognitive development. *Neurotoxicology and Teratology, 13*(4), 357–367.

Conte, R. (1991). Attention disorders. In B. Wong (Ed.), *Learning about learning disabilities* (pp. 60–103). San Diego, CA: Academic Press.

Cox, L. S. (1975). Diagnosing and remediating systematic errors in addition and subtraction computations. *The Arithmetic Teacher, 22,* 151–157.

Cullinan, D. (2002). *Students with emotional and behavioral disorders: An introduction for teachers and other helping professionals.* Upper Saddle River, NJ: Merrill/Prentice Hall.

Curtis, D. (2003). *Ten tips for creating a caring school: Raise your students' emotional intelligence quotient.* Retrieved September 20, 2007, from www.edutopia.org/10-tips-creating-caring-school

Davis, C. J., Knopik, V. S., Olson, R. K., Wadsworth, S. J., & DeFries, J. C. (2001). Genetic and environmental influences on rapid naming and reading ability: A twin study. *Annals of Dyslexia, 51,* 231–247.

Deshler, D. D., Schumaker, J. B., Lenz, B.K., Bulgren, J. A., Hock, M. F., Knight, J., et al. (2001). Ensuring content-area learning by secondary students with learning disabilities. *Learning Disabilities Research & Practice, 16,* 96–108.

Deutsch-Smith, D. (2004). *Introduction to special education: Teaching in an age of opportunity* (5th ed.). Boston: Allyn & Bacon.

Division for Learning Disabilities of the Council for Exceptional Children. (2006). *Teaching students with learning disabilities.* Retrieved August 30, 2007, from www.teachingld.org

Dumas, R. (1994). Early memory loss occurs when offspring's mother exposed to alcohol. *Neurotoxicology and Teratology, 16*(6), 605–612.

Echeverria, D., Heyer, N. J., Martin, M. D., & Naleway, C. A. (1995). Neurological problems among dentists: New concerns for mercury. *Neurotoxicology and Teratology, 17*(2), 161–168.

Emory, E., Patillo, R., Archibold, E., Bayorh, M., & Sung, F. (1999). Neurobehavioral effects of low-level lead exposure in human neonates. *American Journal of Obstetrics and Gynecology, 181*(1), 2–11.

Field, S., & Hoffman, A. (1994). Development of a model for self-determination. *Career Development for Exceptional Individuals, 17,* 159–169.

Field, S., Hoffman, A., & Spezia, S. (1998). *Self-determination strategies for adolescents in transition.* Austin, TX: Pro-Ed.

Fletcher, J. M., Francis, D. J., Shaywitz, S. E., Lyon, G. R., Foorman, B. R., Steubing, K. K., et al. (1998). Intelligent testing and the discrepancy model for children with learning disabilities. *Learning Disabilities Research and Practice, 13*(4), 186–203.

Fletcher, J. M., Lyon, G. R., Barnes, M., Steubing, K. K., Francis, D. J., Olson, R. K., et al. (2002). Classification of learning disabilities: An evidence-based evaluation. In R. Bradley, L. Danielson, & D. P. Hallahan (Eds.), *Identification of learning disabilities: Research to practice* (pp. 185–250). Mahwah, NJ: Lawrence Erlbaum Associates.

Forness, S. R., & Kavale, K. A. (1998). Impact of ADHD on school systems. In P. Jensen & J. R. Cooper (Eds.), *NIH consensus conference on ADHD* (pp. 61–68). Bethesda, MD: National Institutes of Health.

Forness, S. R., & Kavale, K. A. (2001). ADHD and a return to the medical model of special education. *Education and Treatment of Children, 24*(3), 224–247.

Foss, J. M. (2001). *Nonverbal learning disability: How to recognize it and minimize its effects* (ERIC Digest #E619). Arlington, VA: ERIC Clearinghouse on Disabilities and Gifted Education, Council for Exceptional Children. (ERIC Document Reproduction Service No. ED461238)

Fried, P. A., & Smith, A. M. (2001). A literature review of the consequences of prenatal marihuana exposure: An emerging theme of a deficiency in aspects of executive function. *Neurotoxicology and Teratology, 23*(1), 1–11.

Fried, P. A., Watkinson, B., & Gray, R. (1992). A follow-up study of attentional behavior in 6-year-old children exposed prenatally to marihuana, cigarettes, and alcohol. *Neurotoxicology and Teratology, 14*(5), 299–311.

Friend, M. (2005). *Special education: Contemporary perspectives for school professionals.* Boston: Allyn & Bacon.

Fuchs, L. S., Fuchs, D., & Speece, D. L. (2002). Treatment validity as a unifying construct for identifying learning disabilities. *Learning Disability Quarterly, 25*(1), 33–45.

Fuchs, D., Mock, D., Morgan, P., & Young, C. (2003). Responsiveness-to-intervention: Definitions, evidence, and implications for the learning disabilities construct. *Learning Disabilities: Research and Practice, 18*(3), 157–171.

Fulk, B. M., Brigham, F. J., & Lohman, D. A. (1998). Motivation and self-regulation: A comparison of students with learning and behavior problems. *Remedial and Special Education, 19*(5), 300–309.

Gable, R. A., Sugai, G. M., Lewis, T. J., Nelson, J. R., Cheney, D., Safran, S. P., et al. (1997). *Individual and systemic approaches to collaboration and consultation.* Reston, VA: Council for Students with Behavioral Disorders.

Gargiulo, R. M. (2004). *Special education in contemporary society: An introduction to exceptionality.* Belmont, CA: Thompson-Wadsworth.

Geary, D. C., Hamson, C. O., & Hoard, M. K. (2000). Numerical and arithmetical cognition: A longitudinal study of process and concept deficits in children with learning disability. *Journal of Experimental Child Psychology, 77*(3), 236–263.

Gersten, R., Williams, J., Fuchs, L., & Baker, S. (1998). *Improving reading comprehension for children with disabilities: A review of research* (Final Report: Section 1, U.S. Department of Education Contract HS 921700). Washington, DC: U.S. Department of Education.

Gertner, A. B. (2003). *Auditory processing disorders facts.* Retrieved September 10, 2005, from www.homestead.com/agertner/homepage.html

Giler, J. Z. (2000). *Socially ADDept™: A manual for parents of children with ADHD and/or learning disabilities.* Santa Barbara, CA: CES Continuing Education Seminars.

Goodman, Y., & Burke, C. (1972). *Reading miscue inventory manual: Procedure for diagnosis and evaluation.* New York: Macmillan.

Gregg, N., Coleman, C., Stennett, R. B., & Davis, M. (2002). Discourse complexity of college writers with and without disabilities: A multidimensional analysis. *Journal of Learning Disabilities, 35*(1), 23–38.

Gresham, F. M. (1982). Misguided mainstreaming: The case for social skills training with handicapped children. *Exceptional Children, 48*(5), 422–431.

Gresham, F. M. (2002). Responsiveness to intervention: An alternative approach to the identification of learning disabilities. In R. Bradley, L. Danielson, & D. P. Hallahan (Eds.), *Identification of learning disabilities: Research to practice.* Mahwah, NJ: Lawrence Erlbaum Associates.

Gresham, F. M., Sugai, G., & Horner, R. H. (2001). Interpreting outcomes of social skills training for students with high-incidence disabilities. *Exceptional Children, 67,* 331–344.

Gusella, J. L., & Fried, P. A. (1984). Effects of maternal social drinking and smoking on offspring at 13 months. *Neurobehavioral Toxicology and Teratology, 6*(1), 13–17.

Hair, E. C., Jager, J., & Garrett, S. B. (2002). *Helping teens develop healthy social skills and relationships: What research shows about navigating adolescence.* Retrieved September 20, 2007, from www.childtrends.org/Files/K3Brief.pdf

Hallahan, D. P., & Kauffman, J. M. (2003). *Exceptional children: Introduction to special education* (9th ed.). Boston: Allyn & Bacon.

Hallahan, D. P., & Kauffman, J. M. (2006). *Exceptional learners: Introduction to special education* (10th ed.). Boston: Allyn & Bacon.

Hallahan, D. P., Kauffman, J. M., & Lloyd, J. W. (1999). *Introduction to learning disabilities* (2nd ed.). Boston: Allyn & Bacon.

Hansen, D. J., Nangle, D. W., & Meyer, K. A. (1998). Enhancing the effectiveness of social skills interventions with adolescents. *Education and Treatment of Children, 21*(4), 489–513.

Hanson, J. (1992). Fetal alcohol syndrome. *Journal of Pediatrics, 92*(3), 457–460.

Hardman, M. L., Drew, C. J., & Egan, M. W. (2005). *Human exceptionality: Society, school and family* (8th ed.). Boston: Allyn & Bacon.

Henderson, C. (2001). *College freshmen with disabilities, 2001: A biennial statistical profile.* Washington, DC: American Council on Education, Heath Resource Center, ERIC ED458728

Henry, L. A. (2001). How does the severity of a learning disability affect working memory performance? *Memory, 9*(4–6), 233–247.

Heward, W. L. (2005). *Exceptional children: An introduction to special education* (8th ed.). Upper Saddle River, NJ: Prentice Hall.

Holt, S. B., & O'Tuel, F. S. (1989). The effect of sustained silent reading and writing on achievement and attitudes of seventh- and eighth-grade students reading two years below grade level. *Reading Improvement, 26,* 290–297.

Hunt, N., & Marshall, K. (2002). *Exceptional children and youth* (3rd ed.). Boston: Houghton Mifflin.

Hunt, N., & Marshall, K. (2005). *Exceptional children and youth* (4th ed.). Boston: Houghton Mifflin.

Individuals with Disabilities Education Act (IDEA), 34 C.F.R. § 300.7(c)(10) (2004).

Individuals with Disabilities Education Act (IDEA), 34 C.F.R. § 300.18 (2004).

Individuals with Disabilities Education Act (IDEA), 34 C.F.R. § 300.307(1)(3) (2004).

Individuals with Disabilities Education Act (IDEA). 34 C.F.R. § 300.541 (2004).

International Dyslexia Association. (2000). *Dysgraphia.* Retrieved April 10, 2006, from www.interdys.org/ewebeditpro5/upload/Dysgraphia.pdf

International Dyslexia Association. (2007). *What are the signs of dyslexia.* Retrieved February 3, 2008, from www.interdys.org/SignsofDyslexiaCombined.htm

Jenkins, J., & O'Connor, R. (2001, August). *Early identification and intervention for young children with reading/learning disabilities.* Paper presented at the 2001 LD Summit:

Building a Foundation for the Future, Washington, DC. Available online from www.air.org/ldsummit/

John, J. L. (1985). *Basic reading inventory* (3rd ed.). Dubuque, IA: Kendall-Hunt.

Jones, J. (1999). *Dysgraphia accommodations and modifications.* Retrieved September 10, 2005, from www.ldonline.org/ld_indepth/writing/dysgraphia.html

Jongmans, M. J., Smits-Engelsman, B. C. M., & Schoemaker, M. M. (2003). Consequences of comorbidity of developmental coordination disorders and learning disabilities for severity and pattern of perceptual-motor dysfunction. *Journal of Learning Disabilities, 36*(6), 528–537.

Kaplan, D. E., Gayán, J., Ahn, J., Won, T.-W., Pauls, D., Olson, R. K., et al. (2002). Evidence for linkage and association with reading disability. *American Journal of Human Genetics, 70,* 1287–1298.

Kavale, K. A., & Forness, S. R. (1996). Social skill deficits and learning disabilities: A meta-analysis. *Journal of Learning Disabilities, 29,* 226–237.

Kennedy, L., & Mukerji, S. (1986). Ethanol neurotoxicity 2: Direct effects on differentiating astrocytes. *Neurobehavioral Toxicology and Teratology, 8*(1), 17–21.

Kirk, S., Gallagher, J., & Anastasiow, N. (2003). *Educating exceptional children* (10th ed.). Boston: Houghton Mifflin.

Kluwe, R. (1987). Executive decisions and regulation of problem-solving behavior. In F. Weinert & R. Kluwe (Eds.), *Metacognition, motivation and understanding* (pp. 31–64). Hillsdale, NJ: Erlbaum.

Knopik, V. S., Smith, S. D., Cardon, L., Pennington, B., Gayán, J., Olson, R. K., et al. (2002). Differential genetic etiology of reading component processes as a function of IQ. *Behavior Genetics, 32,* 181–198.

Kocchar, C. A., West, L. L., & Haymans, J. M. (2000). *Successful inclusion: Practical strategies for a shared responsibility.* Upper Saddle River, NJ: Prentice Hall.

Kruger, R. J., Kruger, J. J., Hugo, R., & Campbell, N. G. (2001). Relationship patterns between central auditory processing disorders and language disorders, learning disabilities and sensory integration dysfunction. *Communication Disorders Quarterly, 22*(2), 87–99.

Lahm, E. A., & Morrissette, S. K. (1994, April). *Zap 'em with assistive technology: Notetaking, modified materials, assistive writing tools, references, organizational tools, cognitive assistance, adapted access.* Paper presented at the annual meeting of The Council for Exceptional Children, Denver, CO.

LD Online. (n.d.). *LD basics.* Retrieved February 3, 2008, from www.ldonline.org/ldbasics

Learning Disabilities Association. (2005). *Types of learning disabilities.* Retrieved September 10, 2005, from www.ldaamerica.us/aboutld/parents/ld_basics/ types.asp

Learning Disabilities Association of British Columbia. (1997/1998). *Brain development and learning disabilities.* Retrieved September 10, 2005, from www.ldav.ca/articles/ brain_dev.html

Learning Disabilities Roundtable. (2002, July). *Specific learning disabilities: Finding common ground* (A report by the ten organizations participating in the Learning Disabilities Roundtable, sponsored by the Division of Research, Office of Special Education Programs, Department of Education). Washington, DC: Author.

Learning Disabilities Roundtable. (2005, June). *Responsiveness to intervention and learning disabilities* (A report prepared by the National Joint Committee on Learning Disabilities representing 11 national and international organizations). Retrieved August 30, 2007, from www.ldonline.org/?module=uploads&func=download& fileId=461

Leong, C. C., Syed, N. I., & Lorscheider, F. L. (2001). Retrograde degeneration of neurite membrane structural integrity of nerve growth cones following in vitro exposure to mercury. *Neuroreport, 12*(4), 733–737.

Lerner, J. W. (2000). *Learning disabilities: Theories, diagnosis and teaching strategies* (8th ed.). Boston: Houghton Mifflin.

Lerner, J. W. (2002). *Learning disabilities: Theories, diagnosis, and teaching strategies* (9th ed.). Boston: Houghton Mifflin.

Levine, M. D. (1995, July 1). Childhood neurodevelopmental dysfunction and learning disorders. *Harvard Mental Health Letter, 12.*

Library of Congress. (2000). *Project on the decade of the brain.* Retrieved February 3, 2008, from www.loc.gov/loc/brain/

Lucchi, L., & Covelli, V. (1984). Attention deficit disorder (ADD) link brain neurotransmitter dopamine lower after alcohol exposure. *Neurobehavioral Toxicology and Teratology, 6,* 19–24.

Lyon, G. R. (1997). Progress and promise in research in learning disabilities [Electronic version]. *Learning Disabilities: A Multidisciplinary Journal, 8*(1), 1–6.

Lyon, G. R., Fletcher, J. M., Shaywitz, S. E., Shaywitz, B. A., Torgeson, J. K., Wood, F. B., et al. (2001). Rethinking learning disabilities. In C. E. Finn, Jr., A. J. Rotherham, & C. R. Hokanson, Jr. (Eds.), *Rethinking special education for a new century* (pp. 259–287). Washington, DC: Progressive Policy Institute & The Thomas B. Fordham Foundation.

Manzo, K. K., & Zehr, M. A. (1998). Take note. *Education Week, 18*(3), 3.

Marston, D. (2001, August). *A functional and intervention-based assessment approach to establishing discrepancy for students with learning disabilities.* Paper presented at the LD Summit, Washington, DC.

Mattson, S., Riley, P., Jernigan, T. L., Garcia, A., Kaneko, W. M., Ehlers, C. L., et al. (1994). A decrease in the size of the basal ganglia following prenatal alcohol exposure: A preliminary report. *Neurotoxicology and Teratology, 16*(3), 283–289.

Mayes, S. D., Calhoun, S. L., & Cromwell, E. W. (2000). Learning disabilities and ADHD: Overlapping spectrum disorders. *Journal of Learning Disabilities, 33,* 417–424.

Mayo Clinic Staff. (2007a). *Dyslexia.* Retrieved February 1, 2008, from www.mayoclinic.com/health/dyslexia/DS00224

Mayo Clinic Staff. (2007b). *Fetal alcohol syndrome.* Retrieved February 1, 2008, from www.mayoclinic.com/health/fetal-alcohol-syndrome/DS00184

Mazzocco, M. (2001). Advances in research on the fragile X syndrome. *Mental Retardation and Developmental Disabilities Research Reviews, 6*(2), 96–106.

McGrady, H. J., Lerner, J. W., & Boscardin, M. L. (2001). The educational lives of students with learning disabilities. In P. Rodis, A. Garrod, & M. L. Boscardin (Eds.), *Learning disabilities and life stories* (pp. 177–193). Boston: Allyn & Bacon.

McLesky, J. (1992). Students with learning disabilities at primary, intermediate, and secondary grade levels: Identification and characteristics [Electronic version]. *Learning Disability Quarterly, 15,* 13–19.

McLoughlin, J. A., & Lewis, R. B. (1990). *Assessing special students* (3rd ed.). Columbus, OH: Merrill.

Mellard, D. (2004). *Understanding responsiveness to intervention in learning disabilities determination.* Retrieved August 30, 2007, from www.nrcld.org/about/publications/papers/mellard.pdf

Mercer, C. (1997). *Students with learning disabilities* (5th ed.). Upper Saddle River, NJ: Prentice Hall.

Mercer, C. D., Campbell, K. U., Miller, M. D., Mercer, K. D., & Lane, H. B. (2000). Effects of a reading fluency intervention for middle schoolers with specific learning disabilities. *Learning Disabilities Research and Practice, 15,* 179–189.

Merriam-Webster's Collegiate Dictionary (11th ed.). (2006). Springfield, MA: Merriam-Webster.

Moats, L. C. (1994). The missing foundation in teacher education. *Annals of Dyslexia, 44,* 81–102.

National Association of State Directors of Special Education (NASDSE). (2005). *Response to intervention: Policy considerations and implementation.* Alexandria, VA: Author.

National Center for Learning Disabilities. (1999). *Visual and auditory processing disorders.* Retrieved September 10, 2005, from www.ldonline.org/article/6390

National Center for Learning Disabilities. (2004). *LD fast facts.* Retrieved May 19, 2005, from www.schwablearning.org/articles.aspx?g=1&r=627

National Center for Learning Disabilities. (2006). *Dyscalculia.* Retrieved February 3, 2008, from www.ldonline.org/article/13709

National Center for Learning Disabilities. (2008). *Parent center: Dyslexia.* Retrieved February 3, 2008, from www.ncld.org/content/view/454/456173/

National Committee on Science Education Standards and Assessment, National Research Council. (1996). *National science education standards.* Washington, DC: National Academy Press.

National Council of Teachers of Mathematics (NCTM). (2000). *Principles and standards for school mathematics.* Reston, VA: Author.

National Dissemination Center for Children with Disabilities. (2004). *Learning disabilities: Fact sheet 7.* Retrieved September 10, 2005, from www.nichcy.org/pubs/factshe/fs7txt.htm

National Institute of Neurological Disorders and Strokes. (2006). *Dysgraphia information page.* Retrieved April 12, 2006, from www.ninds.nih.gov/disorders/dysgraphia/dysgraphia.htm

National Institute of Neurological Disorders and Strokes. (2007). *Dyslexia information page.* Retrieved February 3, 2008, from www.ninds.nih.gov/disorders/dyslexia/dyslexia.htm

National Institute on Deafness and Other Communication Disorders. (2004). *Auditory processing disorder in children.* Washington, DC: Author. NIH Pub. No. 01–4949. Retrieved February 3, 2008, from www.nidcd.nih.gov/health/voice/auditory.htm

National Joint Committee on Learning Disabilities (NJCLD). (2005). *Responsiveness to intervention and learning disabilities: Concepts, benefits and questions.* Alexandria, VA: Author.

National Research Center on Learning Disabilities (NRCLD). (2006). *Glossary.* Retrieved August 30, 2007, from www.nrcld.org/rti_practices/glossary.html

National Research Council. (2002). *Executive summary: Disproportionate representation of minority students in special education.* Washington, DC: Author.

National Safety Council. (2004). *Lead poisoning.* Retrieved September 10, 2005, from www.nsc.org/library/facts/lead.htm

Neuwirth, S. (1999). *Learning disabilities.* (NIH Publication No. 93-3611) Washington, DC: National Institute of Mental Health. Retrieved September, 10, 2005, from www.healthieryou.com/learn.html

Newman, R. M. (1998). *Gifted & math learning disabled: The dyscalculia syndrome.* Retrieved February 1, 2008, at www.dyscalculia.org/Edu561.html

Nonverbal Learning Disorders Association. (2005). *Welcome to the Nonverbal Learning Disorders Association.* Retrieved September 10, 2005, from www.nlda.org

O'Connor, R., Tilly, D., Vaughn, S., & Marston, D. (2003). *Session 5: How many tiers are needed within RTI to achieve acceptable prevention outcomes and to achieve acceptable patterns of LD identification?* Individual papers presented at National Research Center on Learning Disabilities symposium "Response to Intervention," Kansas City, MO. Available at www.nrcld.org/symposium2003/index.html

Ortiz, S. (2004). *Learning disabilities: A primer for parents about identification* (National Association of School Psychologists Communiqué *32*[5]; NASC Publication HCHS2: S8-117). Available at www.nasponline.org

O'Shaughenessy, T. E., & Swanson, H. L. (1998). Do immediate memory deficits in students with learning disabilities in reading reflect a developmental lag or deficit? *Learning Disability Quarterly, 21,* 123–148.

Pavri, S., & Luftig, R. (2000). The social face of inclusive education: Are students with learning disabilities really included in the classroom? [Electronic version]. *Preventing School Failure, 45*(1), 8–14.

Pavri, S., & Monda-Amaya, L. (2001). Social support in inclusive schools: Student and teacher perspectives. *Exceptional Children, 67,* 391–411.

Pierangelo, R., & Giuliani, G. (2004). Transition services in special education: A practical approach. Boston: Allyn & Bacon.

Pierangelo, R., & Giuliani, G. (2006). *Learning disabilities: A practical approach to foundations, assessment, diagnosis and teaching.* Boston: Allyn & Bacon.

Pierangelo, R., & Giuliani, G. (2007). *Frequently asked questions about Response to Intervention.* Thousand Oaks, CA: Corwin.

Polloway, E. A., Patton, J. R., & Serna, L. (2001). *Strategies for teaching learners with special needs* (7th ed.). Columbus, OH: Merrill.

President's Commission on Excellence in Special Education. (2002). Retrieved May 19, 2005, from www.ed.gov/inits/commissionsboards/whspecialeducation/index.html

Price, B. J., Mayfield, P. K., McFadden, A. C., & Marsh, G. E. (2001). *Teaching: Special education for inclusive classrooms.* Kansas City, MO: Parrot Publishing.

Rawat, A. (1977). Developmental changes in the brain levels of neurotransmitters as influenced by maternal ethanol consumption in the rat. *Journal of Neurochemistry, 28*(6), 1175–1182.

Reschly, D. J., Hosp, J. L., & Schmied, C. M. (2003). *And miles to go . . . : State SLD requirements and authoritative recommendations.* Retrieved July 21, 2005, from www.nrcld.org/about/research/states/index.html

Rivera, D. (1997). Mathematics education and students with learning disabilities: Introduction to special series. *Journal of Learning Disabilities, 30*(1), 2–19, 68.

Rose, D., & Meyer, A. (2000). Universal design for individual differences. *Educational Leadership, 58*(3), 39–43.

Roth, F. P. (2000). Narrative writing: Development and teaching with children with writing difficulties [Electronic version]. *Topics in Language Disorders, 20*(4), 15–28.

Roy, T. S. (1994). Nicotine damages brain cell quality: Effects of prenatal nicotine exposure on the morphogenesis of somatosensory cortex. *Neurotoxicology and Teratology, 16*(40), 1.

Sabornie, E. J., & Kauffman, J. M. (1986). Social acceptance of learning disabled adolescents. *Learning Disabilities Quarterly, 9,* 55–60.

Salend, S. (2001). *Creating inclusive classrooms: Effective and reflective practices.* Upper Saddle River, NJ: Prentice-Hall.

Salvia, J., & Ysseldyke, J. E. (1998). *Assessment* (8th ed.). Boston: Houghton Mifflin.

Scanlon, D., & Mellard, D. F. (2002). Academic and participation profiles of school-age dropouts with and without disabilities. *Exceptional Children, 68,* 239–258.

Schwarzbeck, C. (2000). Chronic disorganization: A bad handicap, unrecognized. Retrieved April 21, 2006, from www.simplyfamily.com/display.cfm?articleID=disorganization.cfm

Scruggs, T. E., & Mastropieri, M. A. (2000). The effectiveness of mnemonic instruction for students with learning and behavior problems: An update and research synthesis. *Journal of Behavioral Education, 10*(2–3), 163–173.

Seligman, M. E. P. (1992). *Helplessness: On depression, development and death.* New York: W. H. Freeman.

Shaywitz, S., & Cohen, D. (1980). Hyperactivity: ADD and behavior disorders linked with alcohol exposure. *Journal of Pediatrics, 96,* 978.

Shinn, M., Walker, H. M., & Stoner, G. (2002). *Interventions for academic and behavioral problems II: Preventive and remedial approaches.* Bethesda, MD: National Association of School Psychologists.

Silver, L. B. (2001). *What are learning disabilities?* Retrieved May 19, 2005, from www.ldonline.org/article/5821.

Smith, C. R. (1998). *Learning disabilities: The interaction of learner, task, and setting* (4th ed.). Boston: Allyn & Bacon.

Smith, S. (1979). *No easy answers.* Cambridge, MA: Winthrop.

Smith, T. E., Polloway, E. A., Patton, J. R., & Dowdy, C. A. (2004). *Teaching students with special needs in inclusive settings.* Boston: Allyn & Bacon.

Spafford, C. A., & Grosser, G. S. (2005). *Dyslexia and reading disabilities: Research and resource guide for working with all struggling readers.* Boston: Allyn & Bacon.

Sridhar, D., & Vaughn, S. (2001). Bibliotherapy for all: Enhancing reading comprehension, self-concept, and behavior. *Teaching Exceptional Children, 33*(2), 74–82.

Stanovich, K. E. (2005). The future of a mistake: Will discrepancy measurement continue to make the learning disabilities field a pseudoscience? *Learning Disabilities Quarterly, 28*(2), 103–106.

Steubing, K. K., Fletcher, J. M., LeDoux, J. M., Lyon, G. R., Shaywitz S. E., & Shaywitz, B. A. (2002). Validity of IQ-discrepancy classification of learning disabilities: A meta analysis. *American Educational Research Journal, 39*(2), 469–518.

Streissguth, A. P., Barr, H. M., & Sampson, P. D. (1986). Attention, distraction and reaction time at age 7 years and prenatal alcohol exposure. *Neurobehavioral Toxicology and Teratology, 8*(6), 717–725.

Sulik, K. K., Johnston, M. C., & Webb, M. A. (1981). Fetal alcohol syndrome: Embryogenesis in a mouse model. *Science, 214*(4523), 936–938. Abstract retrieved September 10, 2005, from www.chem-tox.com/pregnancy/alcohol.htm

Swanson, H. L. (1994). Short-term memory and working memory: Do both contribute to our understanding of academic achievement in children and adults with learning disabilities? *Journal of Learning Disabilities, 27,* 34–50.

Swanson, H. L. (1998). Instructional components that predict treatment outcomes for students with learning disabilities: Support for a combined strategy and direct instruction model. *Learning Disabilities Research and Practice, 14,* 129–140.

Swanson, H. L. (2000). Issues facing the field of learning disabilities [Electronic version]. *Learning Disability Quarterly, 23,* 37–51.

Swanson, H. L., & Hoskyn, M. (1998). Experimental intervention research for students with learning disabilities: A meta-analysis of treatment outcomes. *Review of Educational Research, 68,* 277–321.

Swanson, H. L., & Sachse-Lee, C. (2000). Meta-analysis of single-subject design intervention research for students with LD. *Journal of Learning Disabilities, 33,* 114–136.

Todd, A. W., Horner, R. H., Sugai, G., & Sprague, J. R. (1999). Effective behavior support: Strengthening school-wide systems through a team-based approach. *Effective School Practices, 17*(4), 23–37.

Torgeson, J. K. (1977). The role of nonspecific factors in the task performance of learning disabled children: A theoretical assessment. *Journal of Learning Disabilities, 10,* 27–34.

Torgeson, J. K., & Wagner, R. K. (1998). Alternative diagnostic approaches for specific developmental reading disabilities. *Learning Disabilities Research and Practice, 13,* 220–232.

Tur-Kaspa, H., Weisal, A., & Segev, L. (1998). Attributions for feelings of loneliness of students with learning disabilities. *Learning Disabilities Research and Practice, 13*(2), 89–94.

Turnbull, R., Turnbull, A., Shank, M., & Smith, S. J. (2004). *Exceptional lives: Special education in today's schools* (4th ed.). Upper Saddle River, NJ: Prentice Hall.

University of Maryland Medical Center. (2004). *Learning disabilities: Causes.* Retrieved September 16, 2005, from www.umm.edu/mentalhealth/ldcause.htm

U.S. Department of Education (2000). *The 22nd annual report to Congress on the implementation of Individuals with Disabilities Education Act (IDEA).* Washington, DC: Author.

U.S. Department of Education. (2002). *The 24th annual report to Congress on the implementation of Individuals with Disabilities Education Act (IDEA).* Washington, DC: Author.

U.S. Department of Education. (2004). *The 26th annual report to Congress on the implementation of Individuals with Disabilities Education Act (IDEA).* Washington, DC: Author.

U.S. Office of Education. (1977). *Guide to helping your child understand mathematics.* Boston: Houghton Mifflin.

Vacca, J., Vacca, R., & Grove, M. (1986). *Reading and learning to read.* Boston: Little, Brown.

Vallance, D. D., Cummings, R. L., & Humphries, T. (1998). Mediators of the risk for problem behavior in children with language learning disabilities. *Journal of Learning Disabilities, 31,* 160–171.

Vaughn, S., Elbaum, B., & Boardman, A. G. (2001). The social function of students with learning disabilities: Implications for inclusion. *Exceptionality, 9,* 45–65.

Wadsworth, S. J., Corley, R. P., Hewitt, J. K., Plomin, R., & DeFries, J. C. (2002). Parent offspring resemblance for reading performance at 7, 12 and 16 years of age in the Colorado Adoption Project. *Journal of Child Psychology and Psychiatry, 43*(6), 769–774.

Wakschlag, L., Lahey, B., & Loeber, J. (1997). Smoking during pregnancy increases conduct disorders. *Archives General Psychiatry, 54,* 670–676.

Wehmeyer, M. L., & Schwartz, M. (1997). Self-determination and positive adult outcomes: A follow-up study of youth with mental retardation or learning disabilities. *Exceptional Children, 63,* 245–255.

Winkler, M. (2006). *Causes of learning disabilities and dyslexia: Genetic and biological.* Retrieved February 1, 2008, from http://web4health.info/en/answers/child-learn-biology.htm

Wisconsin Education Association Council. (2007). *Special education inclusion.* Retrieved November 11, 2007, from www.weac.org/resource/june96/speced.htm

Witzel, B., Smith, S. W., & Brownell, M. T. (2001). How can I help students with learning disabilities in algebra? *Intervention in School and Clinic, 37*(2), 101–104.

Wong, B. Y. L. (2000). Writing strategies instruction for expository essays for adolescents with and without learning disabilities. *Topics in Language Disorders, 20*(4), 29–44.

Wood, F. B., & Grigorenko, E. L. (2001). Emerging issues in the genetics of dyslexia: A methodological preview. *Journal of Learning Disabilities, 34,* 503–511.

Worling, D. E., Humphries, T., & Tannock, R. (1999). Spatial and emotional aspects of language inferencing in nonverbal learning disabilities. *Brain and Language, 70,* 220–239.

Wright-Strawderman, C., & Watson, B. L. (1992). The prevalence of depressive symptoms in children with learning disabilities. *Journal of Learning Disabilities, 25,* 258–264.

Zera, D. A., & Lucian, D. G. (2001). Self organization and learning disabilities: A theoretical perspective for the interpretation and understanding of dysfunction [Electronic version]. *Learning Disability Quarterly, 24,* 107–118.

Zins, J. E., Elias, M. J., Weissberg, R. P., Greenberg, M. T., Haynes, N. M., Frey, K. S., et al. (1998). Enhancing learning through social and emotional education. *Think: The Journal of Creative and Critical Thinking, 9,* 18–20. Retrieved August 29, 2007, from www.casel.org/downloads/enhancinglearning.pdf

Index

Academic instruction, 80–91
Age of onset, 8
Annual review, 127–129
Assistive technology, 154–158
Auditory processing disorders, 41–42

Behavioral interventions, 91–96

Causes of learning disabilities, 4–7
  alcohol, 5
  complications during pregnancy, 6
  environmental toxins, 6
  genetics, 4–5
  lead poisoning, 6–7
  maturational delay, 7
  mercury poisoning, 6
  nutrition, 7
  tobacco, 5
Characteristics, 11–12, 14–40
  academic achievement deficits, 16–29
  achievement discrepancy, 31–32
  cognitive deficits, 34
  disorders of attention, 31
  language deficits, 29–30
  memory deficits, 32–34
  metacognition deficits, 34–35
  motivational and attribution
      problems, 39
  perceptual deficits, 40
  social-emotional problems,
      35–38
Classroom accommodations,
  96–98
Comorbidity, 9
Cultural features, 8

Declassification, 129–130
Discrepancy, 9–10
Dyscalculia, 42–44

Dysgraphia, 44–45
Dyslexia, 45–46
Dysorthographia, 46

Educational implications, 12–13
Eligibility criteria, 52–58
Employment services, 142
Exclusionary clause, 10–11

Familial patterns, 8–9

Gender, 8

IDEA, 1–2
IEP committee, 112–121
IEP development, 112–137
Inclusion, 99–111
Individualized transition plan, 141–142

Key facts, 3–4

Least restrictive environment, 121–126

Nonverbal learning disorders,
    38–39, 47–48

Organizational learning
    disorders, 48–49

P.L. 94–142, 2
  Postsecondary education
      options, 148–154
  Prevalence, 7

Response to Intervention, 59–79
  achievement-ability
      discrepancy, 66–67
  events leading to change, 65–66
  fidelity, 77

importance, 61–62
multitiered service delivery
    model, 72–76
parent involvement, 76–77
principles, 62–65
professional development,
    78–79
purpose, 60–61
teachers, 77–78
Role-playing, 105–106

Social cue disorders, 49–50
Social skills, 101–103

Teaching strategies, 80–98
Transition services, 138–158
Triennial review, 129
Types of learning disabilities, 41–51

Visual processing disorders, 50–51
Vocational assessments, 144–147

CORWIN PRESS

The Corwin Press logo—a raven striding across an open book—represents the union of courage and learning. Corwin Press is committed to improving education for all learners by publishing books and other professional development resources for those serving the field of PreK–12 education. By providing practical, hands-on materials, Corwin Press continues to carry out the promise of its motto: **"Helping Educators Do Their Work Better."**